MESSENGERS
TO THE
BRAIN
Our Fantastic Five Senses

By Paul D. Martin
National Geographic Staff

Skyrockets explode in a shower of color. A thrill to see and to hear, fireworks make the Fourth of July a special treat for the senses.

□ BOOKS FOR WORLD EXPLORERS
■ NATIONAL GEOGRAPHIC SOCIETY

Contents

Window on the world: The colored iris of a human eye surrounds the dark pupil. The pupil regulates the amount of light entering the eye. In bright light, muscles in the iris make the pupil smaller, so less light enters the eye. In dim light, the muscles in the iris enlarge the pupil, to admit more light.

CSABA L. MARTONYI/THE W. K. KELLOGG EYE CENTER/THE
UNIVERSITY OF MICHIGAN

COVER: *A puppy's cuddly softness sends messages to the brain of Audrey Lowndes, 10, of Lutherville, Maryland. Audrey feels the soft touch of the puppy through special sense receptors in her skin. Audrey's brain interprets what her sense receptors detect to give her a picture of the world.*

DON CARSTENS

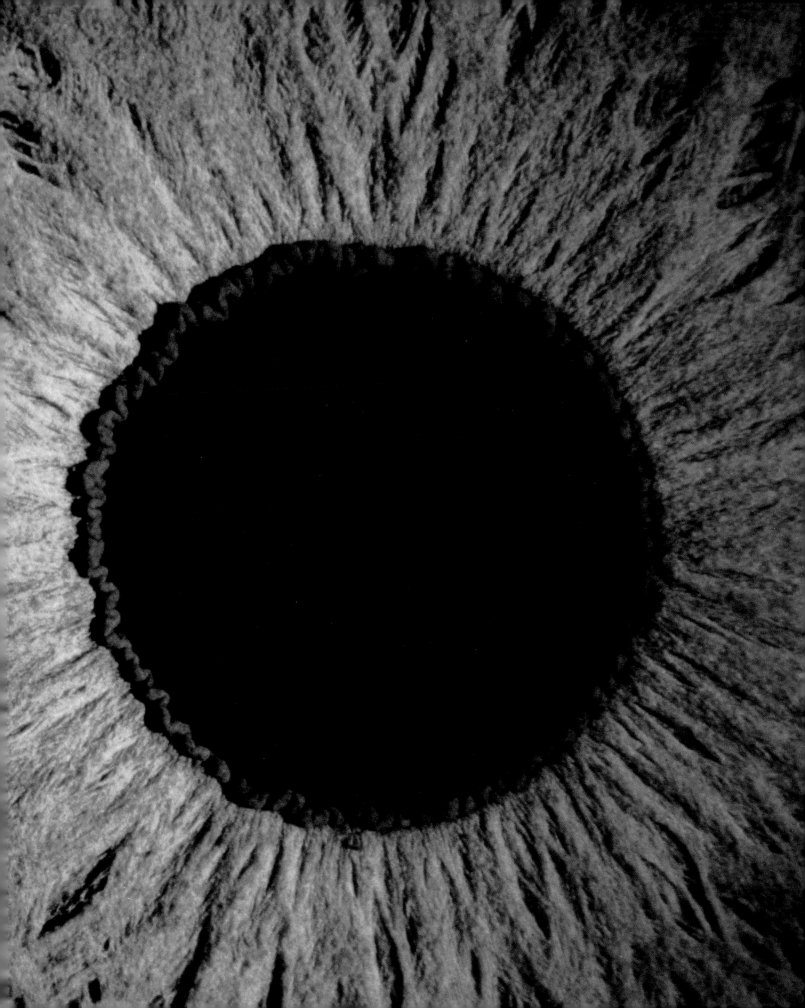

1

Our Fantastic Senses

We depend on them every day—vision, smell, taste, hearing, and touch. Without our five senses, we wouldn't know where we are or what is happening around us. Just think how lost you'd feel if you were suddenly unable to use your senses. For example, imagine that you're exploring a large cave. Your only source of light is a candle flame. As you make your way along a winding passage, the wind snuffs out the candle.

You stand in total darkness, straining to see something. But you can't—not even your hand held close to your face. In the blackness, you hear no sounds. You reach out to touch the side of the cave, but you feel only empty space. You seem to be cut off from the world. Then you remember the matches in your pocket. You strike one, relight your candle, and continue on your way.

For a moment in the cave, you couldn't depend on your senses of vision, hearing, or touch. It was an uncomfortable feeling, one that made you realize how much your senses do for you. They work for you all the time. Your eyes tell you the color of a butterfly's wings. Your nose brings you the scent of a rose. Your fingers feel the softness of a kitten's fur. Your ears bring you the oompah-pah of a tuba playing in a band. Your senses warn you about things that could harm you—lights that could blind you, sounds that could hurt your ears. They warn you when something might be poisonous—or possibly too hot to touch.

As important as the senses are, they are only the beginning of a communications network that allows you to experience and react to things. Your senses flash messages that race along the nerves to the spinal cord and on to the brain. The brain instantly interprets these messages and tells your body how to respond. Like a telegraph system, this network of brain, spinal cord, and nerves operates 24 hours a day. At left and on the following pages you can see some of the ways your senses work for you.

Wonders of the world unfold through the senses. Here Jaime Habel, 10, of Holy Cross, Iowa, peeks at eggs in a bird's nest. Throughout your life, you use your senses to help you discover and understand your world.

JULIE HABEL/WEST LIGHT

Lights swirl on carnival rides at a festival in Calgary, Alberta, in Canada. Your eyes constantly take in information about what is happening around you. They warn you when not to cross the street. They tell you where you can get a sandwich or what's playing at the movies. But your eyes do more than gather useful information. They also allow you to experience a world of pleasurable sights, such as a colorful sunset, stars lighting the sky on a clear night—and the faces of your family and friends.

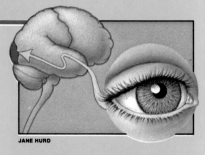

JANE HURD

YOUR EYES, EARS, NOSE, MOUTH, AND SKIN CONTAIN SENSITIVE AREAS CALLED SENSE RECEPTORS. MESSAGES PICKED UP BY THESE RECEPTORS TRAVEL TO SPECIAL AREAS IN THE CEREBRAL CORTEX (SUH-REE-bruhl COR-tex), THE OUTER PART OF THE BRAIN. THIS DRAWING SHOWS WHERE VISUAL MESSAGES GO.

Vision: Sending Images to the Brain

Our eyes gather more information about our surroundings than does any other sense organ. In nearly everything we do—reading, writing, playing—we depend on our eyes.

DAVID FALCONER

Young bikers ride in the Junior Rose Festival Parade (right). Because of its blend of colors, motion, and sounds, a parade puts several senses to work. This event, one of the largest children's parades in the country, takes place each year in Portland, Oregon.

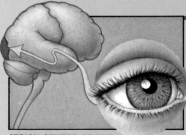

**VISION CENTER OF THE
CEREBRAL CORTEX**

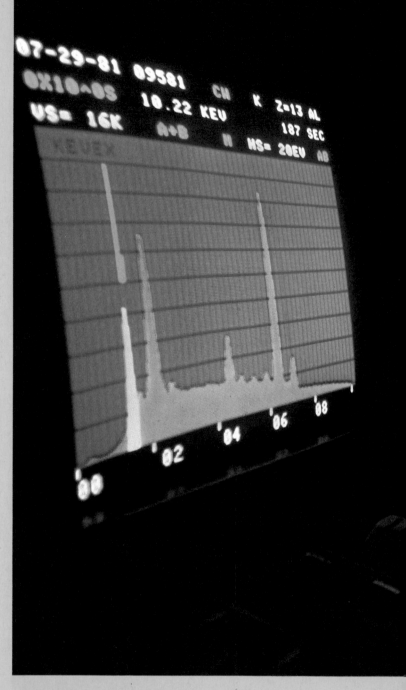

Space shuttle COLUMBIA *soars skyward in a computer-drawn image (below). The computer has added what engineers call a color code. In this image, the different colors show the temperatures of the shuttle and of the surrounding air. The hottest temperature shows as red—the blast of the shuttle's rocket. Other hot areas show as yellow. Cooler areas show as blue or black. Computer images like this are called thermograms. This one proved to scientists that the shuttle did not get too hot or too cold during flight.*

Looking beneath the surface, a metals specialist at Rockwell International, in Troy, Michigan (above), works with a computer and a powerful magnifier called an electron microscope. He uses these devices to check for defects in a metal sample. Scientists and other professionals depend on machines like these to help them see things they cannot see with the unaided eye. Using computers, engineers can draw pictures of things that do not yet exist, such as a design for a new car.

HOWARD SOCHUREK

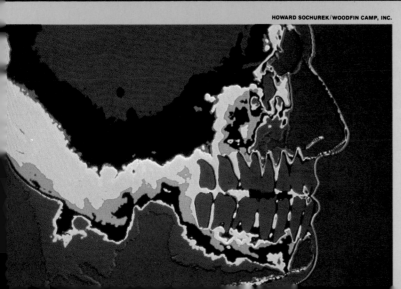

Bright colors give another kind of information in an image of a human head (left). These colors indicate how dense, or concentrated, the different parts of the head are. Harder parts, such as the skull and the teeth, show up as red. Softer parts, such as the nose and the throat, show up as dark blue. If certain colors appear in unusual places, they can sometimes indicate to doctors why a person is sick. This image is called a density scan. A computer created it by giving different colors to the shades of gray on a black-and-white X ray.

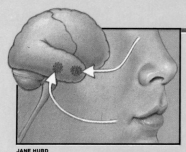

JANE HURD

TASTE (MAGENTA) AND SMELL
(PURPLE) CENTERS OF THE
CEREBRAL CORTEX

Our Senses of Taste and Smell

These two senses work separately and have different pathways to the brain. When you eat, the two senses work together. Without both, you wouldn't enjoy your food.

In the test kitchen of McCormick and Co., Inc., a spice company in Baltimore, Maryland, young tasters sample spaghetti sauce from a pot (below). Tracey Manning, 10, left, and her sister Jeannine, 13, of Towson, Maryland, are helping the company test a new recipe.

The testers lick their lips as Carolyn Manning, a manager at McCormick, slides the finished spaghetti from the oven. Enjoyment of food begins with judging its smell—and its looks. When you eat, tiny sensors in your mouth called taste buds detect different tastes. A food's flavor also depends on its aroma. Other testers are Lisa Stokes, 10, and Charles Muse, 11, right, of Baltimore, and Jamie Furman, 10, of Towson.

SUSAN T.MCELHINNEY (BOTH)

Spicy treat: Carrie Reaser, 10, gets set to bite into a hot dog at Huntington Beach, California. Catsup and mustard add to the flavor of Carrie's hot dog. Your taste buds recognize only four basic sensations—sour, salty, sweet, and bitter. These four sensations combine with the aromas detected by your sense of smell to produce the many flavors you experience.

PIERRE KOPP/WEST LIGHT

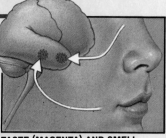

As their mother turns a fried egg, Bryan, left, and Erin Harvey enjoy the smells of an outdoor breakfast (above). The sense of smell is far more sensitive than the sense of taste. Most people can identify a substance after smelling a few particles of it. But they need many more particles to allow them to taste that substance. Bryan, 7, and Erin, 3, live in Richmond, Virginia.

Lauren Wigo, 6, of New York City, discovers that roasting a marshmallow changes its taste and its texture (right). Marshmallows and other sweet foods taste good to most of us from birth. Many people learn to like the flavors of foods that they may have disliked at first, such as liver or spinach. But most never learn to like certain tastes. Many poisons, for example, taste bitter. Our natural dislike of such flavors warns us not to swallow bitter substances.

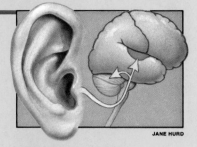

HEARING (DARK GREEN) AND BALANCE (LIGHT GREEN) CENTERS OF THE BRAIN

Hearing and Balance

Your sense of hearing helps you communicate through speech. In addition to hearing receptors, your ears contain organs that help your brain give you a sense of balance.

Sharing her book, Elizabeth deGrazia reads to Alexandra Steedman, 13, in a park on Staten Island, New York (left). Your ears take in thousands of sounds every day. Your brain, however, screens out some of them. Although cars may be moving nearby, Alexandra may not be aware of them as she listens to Elizabeth.

Mandy Datisman whispers a joke to her sister Brandi in their backyard in Sherrill, Iowa (above). Mandy, 13, and Brandi, 8, can talk to each other thanks to hearing. People who become deaf after learning to talk can still speak afterward. But people born deaf have a difficult time learning to talk. That's because we learn to talk by imitating speech we hear.

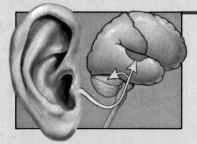

HEARING (DARK GREEN) AND
BALANCE (LIGHT GREEN) CENTERS
OF THE BRAIN

Moving to the beat: Rhonda Fangman, 9, and Karie Ann Krogman, 14, dance to a song from a portable radio (below). Without the sense of hearing, they could not enjoy the music. Hearing does more than allow people to listen to music or to talk with one another. It also helps protect them. It brings them sounds of warning, such as auto horns, sirens, and fire alarms.

JULIE HABEL

RICHARD HOWARD/BLACK STAR

As her dog, Sam, listens intently, Laurel Bennert Ohlson plays the French horn (above). Laurel is a member of the National Symphony Orchestra, in Washington, D.C. She says Sam likes to listen to her play. Many animals have sharper hearing than that of humans. But a musician's ear is sensitive enough to pick out a single instrument being played in a large orchestra.

Music means more than fun to Indians of the Santa Clara Pueblo, in New Mexico. Eddy Kabotie, 7, helps beat out a rhythm for dancers during a religious ceremony honoring the village patron saint. Music is an important part of the religious and social activities of many people around the world.

Trailing by a tail, Eddie Cummer, 6, holds onto Thunder, the family pony. Eddie's sister and two brothers—Sallie, 10, Russel, 11, and Gregory, 3—share a ride. The Cummer children are on their family's farm, near Sherrill, Iowa. The youngsters probably don't realize it, but their ears help them ride Thunder. A part of the ear sends signals to the brain telling it where the head is in relation to the ground. The brain then calls into action the muscles needed to maintain balance.

JULIE HABEL

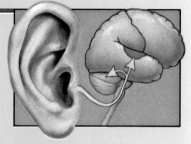

HEARING (DARK GREEN) AND BALANCE (LIGHT GREEN) CENTERS OF THE BRAIN

Hearing and Balance

In addition to enabling you to hear, your ears contain organs of balance. These organs signal your brain when your head moves in any direction.

Hands-down winner: Sally Smith, of Shelburne, Vermont, completes her first handstand. The feat surprised her father. "He didn't think I could do it on the first try," she says. Signals sent to Sally's brain from inside her ears helped her balance on her hands.

CLYDE H. SMITH/PETER ARNOLD, INC.

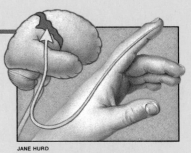

TOUCH CENTER OF THE CEREBRAL CORTEX

Touch: Messages of Feeling

Sense receptors in your skin allow you to feel the world around you. In addition to the experience of touch, these receptors enable you to feel pain, warmth, and coolness.

Sharing a happy moment, Kelly Tauke, 4, and her 8-year-old sister Tracy, hug their mother at their home, near Guttenberg, Iowa (left). Humans often show affection by touching. Some areas of the body, such as the lips, are more sensitive to touch than others. That's why a kiss feels good.

"Cold and wet" is how a frog's skin feels, according to Tim Lougher, of Honeoye Falls, New York (above). Tim, 11, found the frog in a pond. Your skin contains many sense receptors. You also have sense receptors inside your body that tell your brain what is happening there.

"W-Want to join us for a l-little s-s-swim?" Members of a swimming group in the Soviet Union rub themselves with snow. They are trying to prepare their bodies for a swim in the ice-cold Moscow River, in Moscow. Most people wouldn't enjoy such an activity. But we all feel other exciting sensations every day, from romping with a puppy to taking that first bicycle ride—all thanks to our fantastic five senses.

CARL MYDANS/BLACK STAR

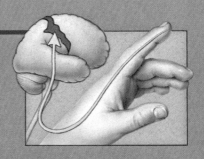

TOUCH CENTER OF THE CEREBRAL CORTEX

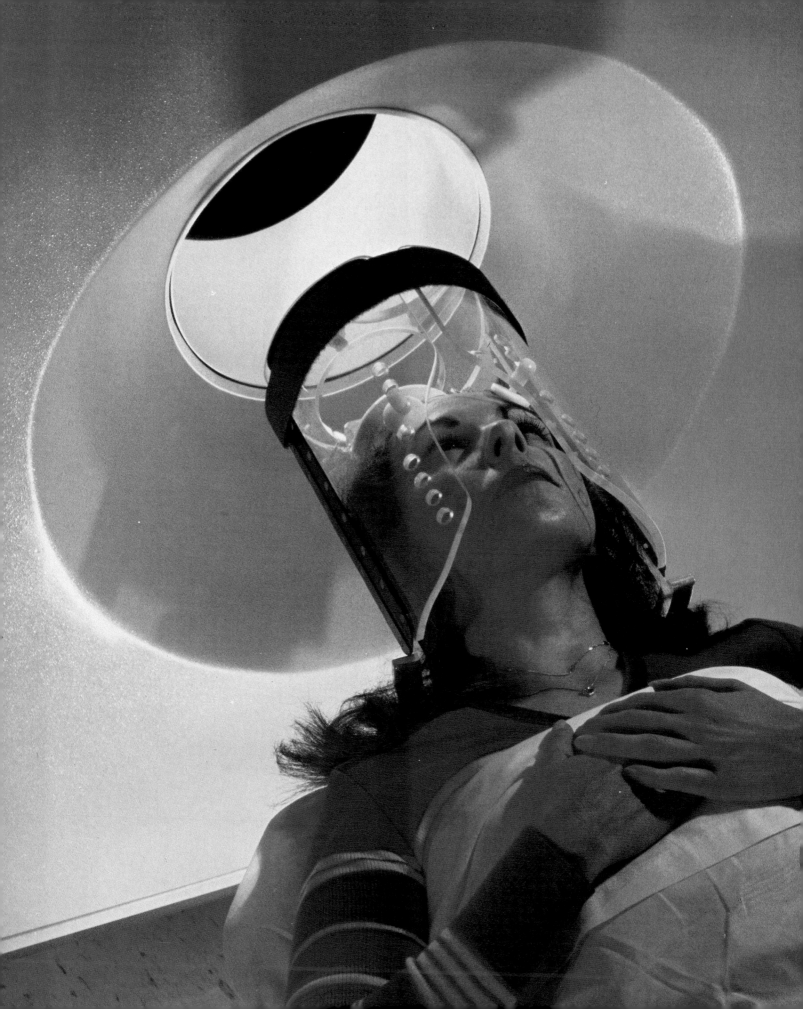

2

The Central Nervous System

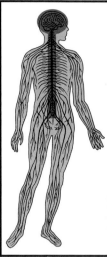

Your brain is the most precious part of your body. It's what helps make you—you! A vast storage facility, your brain records as memories everything you experience. Your every thought and feeling depend upon your brain. In fact, the complexity of your brain is what makes you a human being. It lets you communicate with other people through language. It causes you to feel joy or sadness. It enables you to solve problems, to move—and to think about the future.

The brain also serves as your body's main control center. It is the most important part of the internal communications network known as the nervous system. Besides the brain, the nervous system consists of the spinal cord and a network of nerve fibers that reach out from the brain and spinal cord to every part of the body. The brain and spinal cord together form the central nervous system.

More complex and efficient than any computer, your brain constantly receives information from your senses about what is happening outside and inside your body. The messages travel in the form of electro-chemical impulses —electric currents helped on by chemical substances. The brain instantly analyzes this information and sends out impulses that order your body into action and help keep it operating smoothly.

The spinal cord acts as a pipeline for most of the information entering and leaving the brain. The spinal cord receives information from the areas of the body below the neck and sends out commands for movement. Information from the head goes directly to the brain. Without the brain and spinal cord to interpret and respond to signals from the senses, the senses themselves would be useless. It would be as if a TV station were broadcasting a program but there were no TV sets at the other end to receive it.

THE NERVOUS SYSTEM IS THE BODY'S INTERNAL COMMUNICATIONS NETWORK. IT CONSISTS OF THE BRAIN, THE SPINAL CORD, AND THE NERVES THAT SPREAD THROUGHOUT THE BODY.

SUSAN SANFORD

World's most mysterious object: The human brain reveals its wrinkled surface in a computer-drawn image (below). For centuries, people have tried to understand the brain. Only recently have scientists begun to discover some of the secrets that reveal how this complicated organ operates.

HOWARD SOCHUREK

A space-age instrument helps scientists look into the brain (left). This woman is waiting to be examined with a machine called a PET *scanner.* PET *stands for positron emission tomography. The scanner measures different levels of activity in the brain. A computer then assigns a color to each level and shows it on a TV screen. Doctors can study the images to see details inside the woman's brain. The* PET *scanner is just one of several new tools doctors use to study the brain.*

© ROGER RESSMEYER/STARLIGHT

25

Exploring the Brain

If you could travel inside a human brain, you'd be in for quite a trip. The brain is the most amazing part of the human body. It is also the most complex object known in the universe.

Some people think of the brain as a single solid object inside the head. But it's really made up of several parts. Three main parts are the brain stem, the cerebellum (sehr-uh-BELL-um), and the cerebrum (suh-REE-brum). Each part performs special jobs.

The brain stem controls the actions of your internal organs, such as the heart and the lungs. It works whether you are asleep or awake. It also serves as a relay station between parts of the brain and the rest of the nervous system. Messages from the body travel up the spine into the brain stem. A part of the brain stem sorts and analyzes these signals and relays them to other parts of the brain.

Behind the brain stem is the cerebellum. Its job is to control posture and to coordinate the muscles during movement. Say you decide to tie your shoelaces. Your cerebellum helps you accomplish this by coordinating your fingers so they work together smoothly.

The most important part of the brain is the cerebrum. It is divided into two hemispheres, or halves. These make up about two-thirds of the brain. Your thoughts occur in the cerebrum and your memories are stored there. It's the area where most learning takes place.

Scientists have found that the left cerebral hemisphere controls the right side of the body, and the right cerebral hemisphere controls the left side of the body. The two hemispheres also seem to control different types of mental activity. The left hemisphere controls reasoning skills, such as those used in language and math. The right hemisphere controls the emotions and the ability to see things as a whole rather than in parts.

(Continued on page 28)

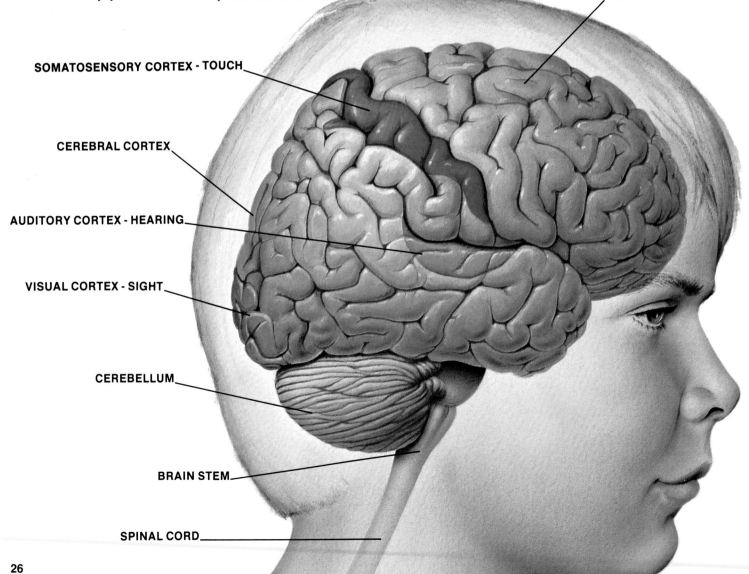

CEREBRUM

SOMATOSENSORY CORTEX - TOUCH

CEREBRAL CORTEX

AUDITORY CORTEX - HEARING

VISUAL CORTEX - SIGHT

CEREBELLUM

BRAIN STEM

SPINAL CORD

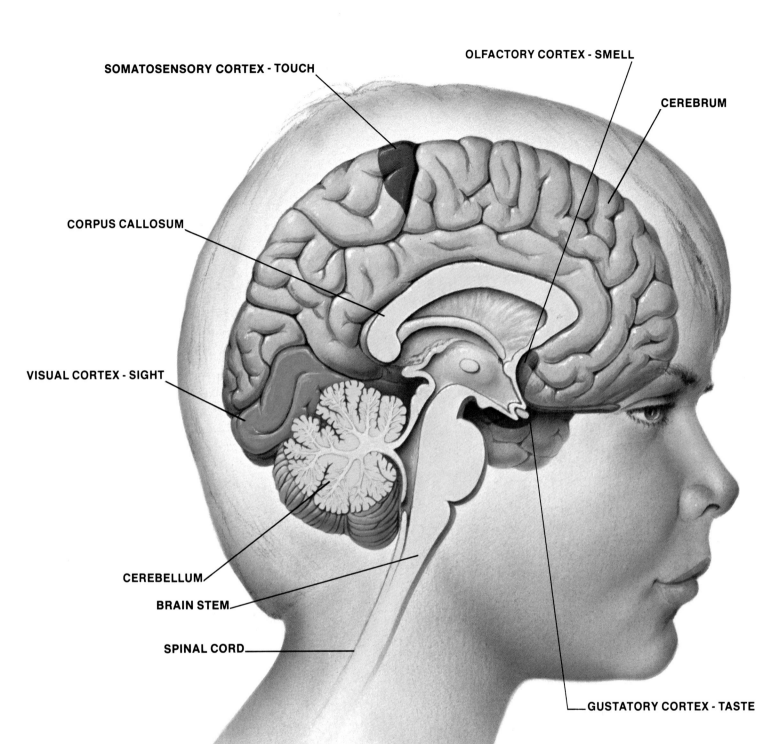

SOMATOSENSORY CORTEX - TOUCH

OLFACTORY CORTEX - SMELL

CEREBRUM

CORPUS CALLOSUM

VISUAL CORTEX - SIGHT

CEREBELLUM

BRAIN STEM

SPINAL CORD

GUSTATORY CORTEX - TASTE

JANE HURD

Chalkboard of the mind. Messages from the senses travel along the nerves to the thin outer layer of the brain, the cerebral cortex. This layer is only a fraction of an inch thick. But, because of its many convolutions, or folds, it has a large surface. Some senses "write" their messages in a specific area of the cerebral cortex. The drawing at left shows the primary sensory areas in which messages of touch, hearing, and vision are recorded. The brain's inner structure has specialized parts that perform different jobs. The drawing above shows the brain as if it were cut down the center. The brain stem connects the brain and the spinal cord. The cerebellum is responsible for controlling posture—holding the position of the body in space—and for muscle coordination. The corpus callosum (kah-LOW-sum) joins the left and right halves of the brain. The cerebral cortex is part of the largest area of the brain, the cerebrum. Messages that reach the primary sensory areas of the cerebral cortex then go to other areas in the cortex. There, they are combined with messages from other senses to form a total experience.

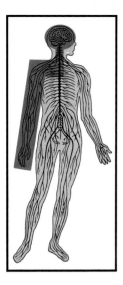

THE CENTRAL NERVOUS SYSTEM AND THE NERVES THAT SPREAD OUT FROM IT REGULATE THE ENTIRE BODY.

(Continued from page 26)

The outer surface of the cerebrum is called the cerebral cortex. It consists of a thin, grayish layer of nerve cells. Certain areas of the cerebral cortex receive information gathered by your eyes, your ears, and touch receptors on every part of your body. Another area, the motor cortex, sends out messages that control all your voluntary movements—the movements you decide to make.

The largest part of the cerebral cortex consists of association areas. Scientists believe that the association areas help coordinate and process information sent to the brain by the senses. Although much remains unknown about them, the association areas probably are where thought and understanding occur. Association areas in some parts of the cortex may be concerned with memory. Areas in other locations may be involved with interpreting the meaning of words.

Here's an example of how the association areas might work: You hear a flutter nearby and turn your eyes toward the sound. The sound flashes to one part of your brain. What you see—a tiny flying object—goes to a different area. In an instant, association areas in your cortex compare the sound and sight with things you've read and seen and tell you "hummingbird."

On these and the next pages, you'll see how messages travel from all parts of your body to your brain. Then you'll see brain cells and find out how they communicate with each other.

The touch of a calf's nose (right) sets off a chain reaction. As the calf nudges Tracy Tauke, touch-pressure receptors—areas sensitive to touch—in Tracy's finger send signals along nerve fibers into the spinal cord and on to the brain. The nerve cells in Tracy's brain interpret the signals, telling her that the calf's nose feels cool and wet.

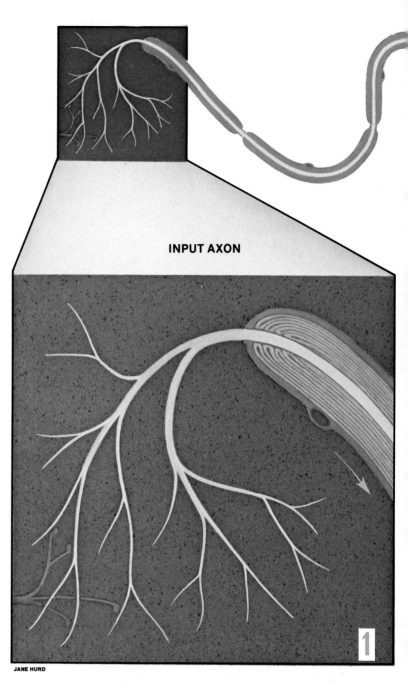

INPUT AXON

1

JANE HURD

JULIE HABEL

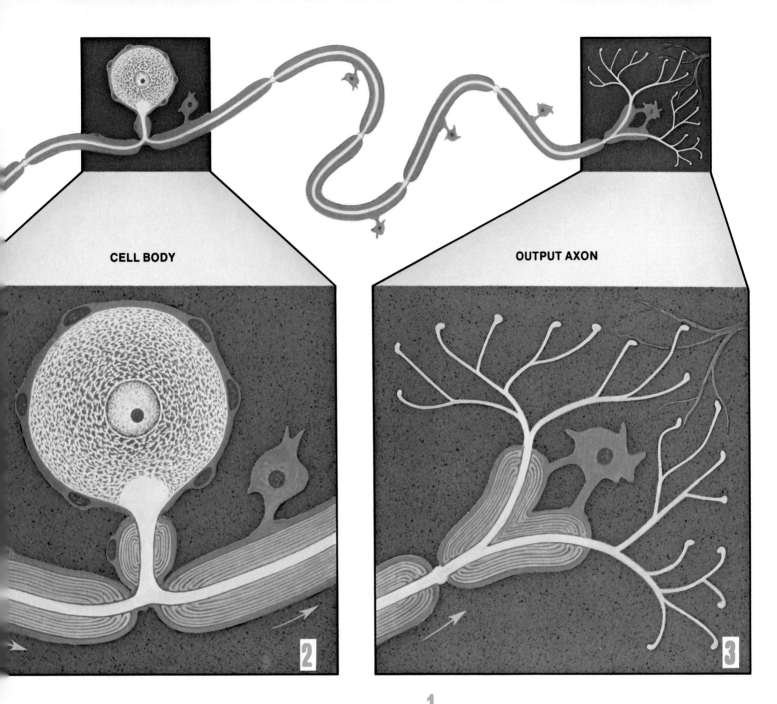

CELL BODY

OUTPUT AXON

![2]

![3]

Building block of the nervous system, *the nerve cell called the neuron carries the messages that cause the body to function. The messages travel in the form of tiny electrical impulses. There are many types of neurons. Some carry impulses from the sense organs to the brain. Others carry impulses from the brain or spinal cord to the muscles and internal organs. Still others do their work entirely within the central nervous system. The neuron in the drawings above transmits nerve impulses from the sensory receptors, such as those in the skin, to the neurons in the spinal cord. The top drawing shows what this type of nerve cell looks like. The three large drawings show the cell's main parts—the input axon (ACK-sahn), the cell body, and the output axon.*

1 *The input axon has ends that branch out much the way tree roots do. When Tracy's finger sends nerve impulses, these branches pick them up.*

2 *The ball-shaped cell body receives the impulses from the input axon and sends them on to the output axon. Small glia (GLEE-uh) cells attached to the axons and the cell body support the neuron. Some produce a covering that electrically insulates the axons.*

3 *The output axon also may have many branches at its tip. Each branch ends in a small knob, or terminal. The point at which a terminal of the output axon communicates with other nearby neurons is called a synapse (SIN-aps). The impulses cross the synapse and continue along the next neuron.*

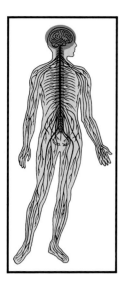

THE PERIPHERAL (PUH-RIFF-UH-RUHL) NERVES SPREAD THROUGHOUT THE BODY. THEY CARRY MESSAGES TO AND FROM THE CENTRAL NERVOUS SYSTEM.

Neurons and Nerves

How does your brain keep track of what's happening all over your body? It relies on a network of nerves that connect the sensory receptors throughout the body. This network is known as the peripheral nervous system. Peripheral nerves carry impulses to your spinal cord and brain.

Without the peripheral nervous system to link it to the body, the central nervous system would be much like a king trapped in a castle and cut off from the world. Peripheral nerves provide the central nervous system with the information it needs to run its "kingdom."

Twelve pairs of nerves branch out from the brain. Thirty-one additional pairs extend from the spinal cord. Nerves that carry messages to the brain and spinal cord are known as sensory nerves. They carry incoming signals from sense receptors in the eyes, the ears, and all other parts of your body. Nerves that carry messages away from the central nervous system are called motor nerves. They transmit commands that cause muscles to contract and organs to function.

The peripheral nervous system also contains autonomic (aht-uh-NAHM-ik) nerves. Autonomic nerves, like motor nerves, carry messages from the central nervous system to other parts of the body. Motor nerves carry messages that control things you do on purpose, such as jumping or walking. Autonomic nerves carry messages that control actions occurring automatically within your body, such as the inflating of your lungs when you breathe or the opening or closing of your blood vessels.

Nerve impulses travel at different speeds in different kinds of nerve fibers. A covering of a fatty substance called myelin (MY-uh-luhn) helps increase the speed of impulses. In nerves with this covering, impulses may travel as fast as 300 feet a second (91 m/s).* In nerves without it, they may travel only 3 or 4 feet a second (91-122 cm/s).

*Metric figures in this book have been rounded off.

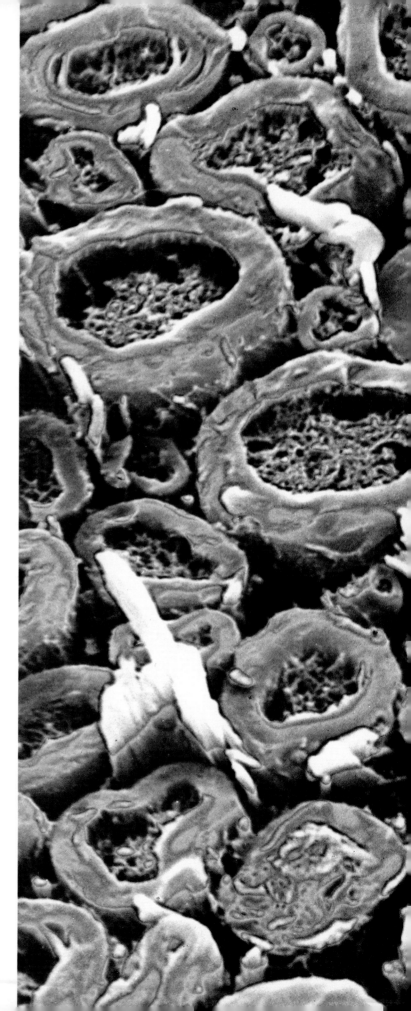

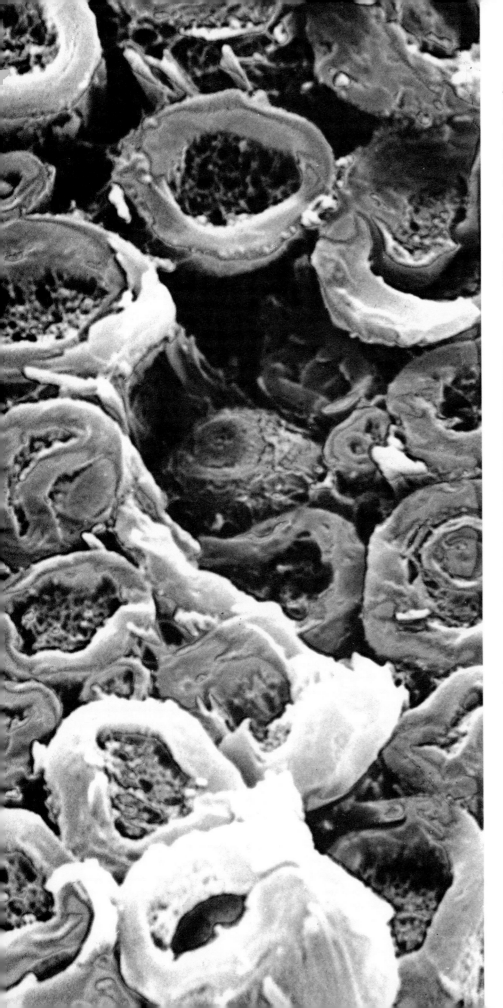

Nerve fibers resemble telephone wires inside a cable (left). Nerve fibers carry information to or from the central nervous system. They consist of long, threadlike axons branching out from nerve cells in the brain and spinal cord. Glia cells wrap some axons in myelin, a substance that helps increase the speed of nerve impulses. A group of axons forms a single nerve bundle. This nerve bundle has been enlarged 2,775 times.

FROM *TISSUES AND ORGANS:A TEXT-ATLAS OF SCANNING ELECTRON MICROSCOPY* BY RICHARD G. KESSEL AND RANDY H. KARDON. W. H. FREEMAN AND COMPANY. COPYRIGHT © 1979

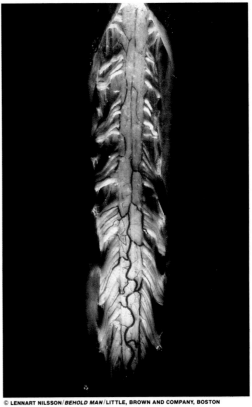

The brain's chief link with the rest of body, the spinal cord (above) runs from the head to the lower back. The backbone surrounds and protects this delicate communication cable. Thirty-one pairs of nerves are connected to the spinal cord. This photograph shows nerves entering the back of the cord. These carry signals into the spinal cord. Other nerves entering at the front carry signals away from the spinal cord.

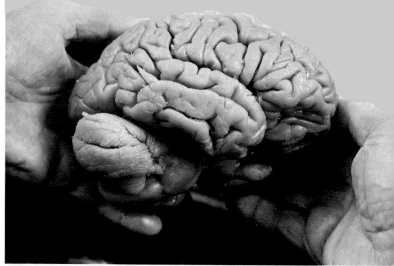

Wrinkled as a walnut, the adult human brain (right) weighs about 3 pounds (1½ kg). During a baby's first few months of life, its brain weighs about 1 pound (½ kg). The brain reaches its full size by the time a person is 6 years old. This model was made from a cast taken of a real brain. The view shows the right side of the brain. The brain actually has a pinkish-gray color. It is 85 percent water and so soft it would lose its shape without the skull to contain it. Because the brain works so hard, it needs plenty of nourishment. This important organ makes up only about 2 percent of the body's weight. But it uses nearly 20 percent of the body's supply of oxygen.

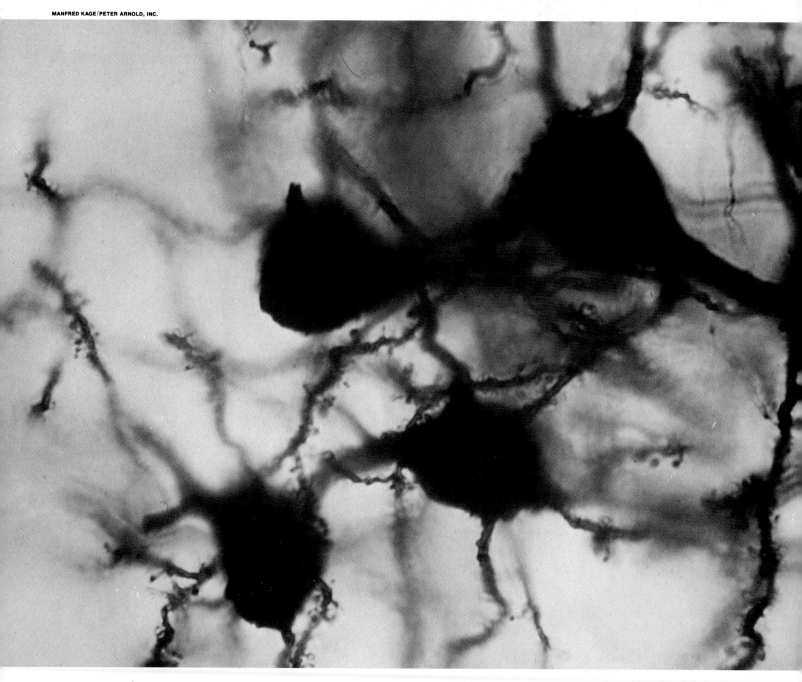

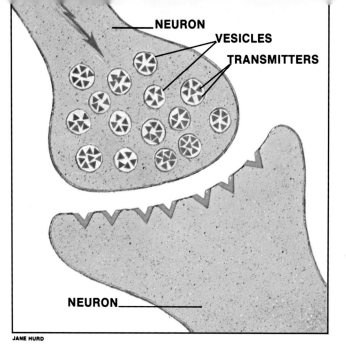

NEURON

VESICLES

TRANSMITTERS

NEURON

JANE HURD

Nerve cells interlock to form a web of communication in the brain (below). These neurons act as "go-betweens" in sending and receiving impulses. If you look closely, you'll see that each cell consists of a pyramid-shaped cell body and many fine threads, with one thread longer than the others. The shorter threads, called dendrites (DEN-drites), carry impulses into the cell body. The longer thread, known as the axon, carries impulses from the cell body to other neurons. Neurons form countless nerve pathways in the brain. The neurons in this photograph have been enlarged 1,200 times. A colored stain has been added to help make them easier to see.

Nerve-cell language: The drawings above and below show how a nerve impulse passes from one neuron to another. The region where neurons relay impulses is called a synapse. Impulses travel through neurons as electrical currents. Most travel across synapses as chemical messages. Above, an electrical impulse nears the terminal of a nerve fiber. The tip of the fiber has many tiny sacs known as vesicles (VEH-sih-kuhls). They contain chemicals called transmitters. When the electrical impulse reaches the terminal (below), the vesicles release their chemicals into the synaptic cleft—the small gap between the two neurons. The chemical messengers cross the gap and lock into receptors in the receiving cell. There the chemicals generate a new electrical signal.

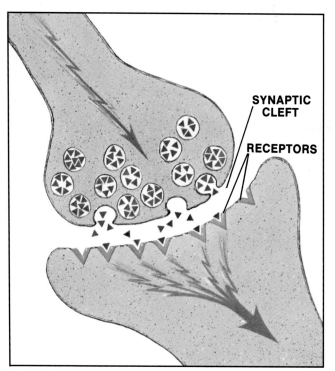

SYNAPTIC CLEFT

RECEPTORS

The Brain's Communications Network

Information from the sensory receptors in your head and neck, including those in your eyes, nose, and ears, goes directly to your brain. Information from receptors in the rest of your body travels first to the spinal cord. The spinal cord consists of a core of "gray matter"—nerve cells and glia—with a wrapping of "white matter"—nerve fibers. Thick bundles of nerve fibers, called fiber tracts, work constantly to carry impulses back and forth between your brain and the rest of your body.

Except for smell messages, all sensory information passes through the thalamus (THALL-uh-muss), a kind of processing center.

From the thalamus, the signals go to the sensory areas of the cerebral cortex that you saw on page 26, and to other areas within the brain where such information is processed and analyzed.

Inside the brain, billions of nerve cells intermesh in a thick tangle of communication. Although each nerve cell works separately, one cell can communicate with many other cells through synapses. Individual nerve cells in the brain communicate with hundreds—or perhaps thousands—of other cells.

The brain is many times more complicated than any machine ever invented. Scientists estimate that there may be a hundred billion nerve cells in the brain.

You were born with nearly all the brain cells you'll ever have. Some of these cells die as you age. But don't worry about running out of room to store all your experiences. Even if you live to be a hundred, you'd never come close to using all the cells in your brain.

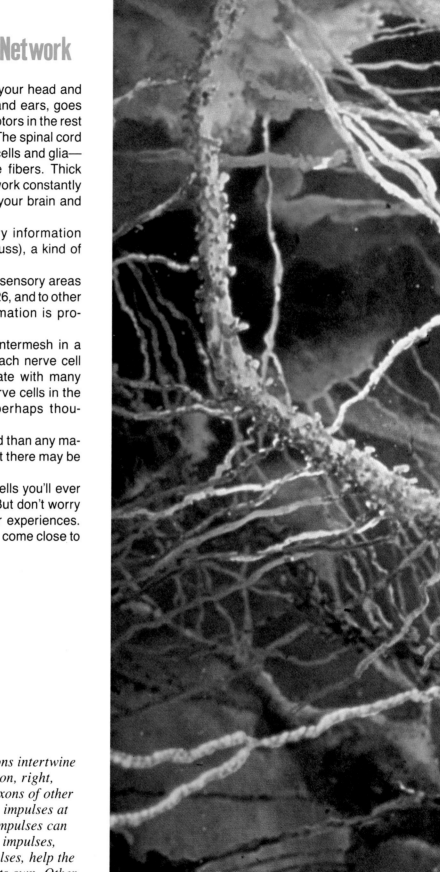

Like tangled vines, nerve fibers from neurons intertwine in the brain. In this painting, the blue neuron, right, receives impulses from orange and white axons of other brain cells. A neuron can receive incoming impulses at many points on its surface. The incoming impulses can affect the neuron in one of two ways. Some impulses, called excitatory (ex-SYE-tuh-toh-ree) impulses, help the neuron to trigger an electrical impulse of its own. Other incoming impulses, called inhibitory (in-HIB-uh-toh-ree) impulses, make it more difficult for the neuron to trigger an impulse.

Watching the Brain at Work

As you read these words, your nervous system is alive with activity. Receptors in your eyes are busily changing patterns of light into nerve impulses. These impulses zip along nerve pathways to the cerebral cortex. There the impulses are interpreted as letters, words, and images.

Even the simplest activities cause countless neurons to signal to each other. Like millions of fireflies flashing in the night, the neurons in your brain are constantly turning on and off as nerve impulses race through your mind.

Activities such as reading or listening to music use cells in different parts of the brain. In recent years, scientists have developed a test that shows the brain at work. This test is called the PET scan. A PET scan actually shows the brain—or other part of the body—while it is functioning.

To make a PET scan of the brain, doctors give the person to be tested a special solution of sugar—the brain's fuel. The PET scanner detects the rate at which different parts of the brain "burn" or use up the sugar. A computer attached to the PET scanner shows the activity as different colors on a TV screen.

The pictures on this page show how the brain appears when a person is at rest and while a person is listening to speech. Pictures on the opposite page show the brain when a person is listening to music and when that person is listening to speech and music at the same time. Areas with a lot of activity show as red and yellow. Areas with little activity show as blue and green.

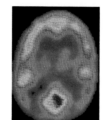

Color-coded image of a PET scan (left) shows the brain at work. Russell Hoeger, 10, of New Vienna, Iowa, covers his ears (below). At left, you can see how Russell's brain would look on a PET scan. The red spot at the back of the brain, shown here at the bottom, indicates that the eyes are open and the visual cortex is active.

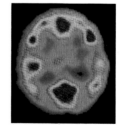

A few words from his friend Rhonda Fangman (far left) creates activity in Russell's brain. On a PET scan, Russell's brain would look like this: A red spot would form on the left of the brain. For most people, spoken language is analyzed by the left side of the brain. Scientists believe that the spot at the front of the brain, shown here at the top, indicates that the language has brought the brain's imagination and planning powers into action.

COMPUTER IMAGES: COURTESY OF DRS. MICHAEL E. PHELPS AND JOHN C. MAZZIOTTA

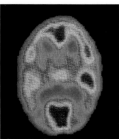

Russell listens to music on a portable radio (right). A PET *scan of his brain now would show that, along with the imagination and planning center, the hearing center on the right side of the brain is active. Most people use the right side of the brain when they listen to music.*

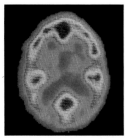

As Russell listens to music, Rhonda talks to him (below). A PET *scan of his brain would show the sides, the front, and the back lit up. Tests such as this help scientists learn more about how your brain receives and interprets messages from your sense receptors.*

PHOTOGRAPHS: JULIE HABEL

3

Vision: Sending Images to the Brain

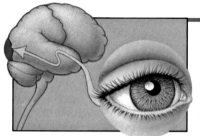

RAYS OF LIGHT ENTERING THE EYE BECOME ELECTRICAL IMPULSES. THESE TRAVEL TO THE VISUAL CORTEX, THE AREA OF THE BRAIN IN WHICH THEY ARE INTERPRETED AS VISION.

A pink balloon floats in a deep blue sky. A bright yellow flower rests in an orange vase. A white chicken pecks in the dust beside a red barn.

Sights such as these are so common that you may not pay much attention to them. But each of these sights is actually part of a miracle—the miracle of vision. Because of vision you can see light from a star billions of miles away. With a single glance you can detect a grain of sand or see the tallest building in the world.

Vision tells you the size and shape of objects, how near they are, and how fast they are moving. With your eyes, you can see the dozens of small black lines that make up the letters of these words.

You depend on vision more than on any other sense to help you find out about the world each day. Your eyes work every minute you're awake. Whether you're reading, writing, watching television, playing a fast game of basketball, or simply walking down the street, your eyes are busy.

Your eyes and other sense organs work because of billions of nerve cells known as sense receptors. Sense receptors in your skin, mouth, nose, and ears, as well as in your eyes, constantly gather information from the outside world. However, not all sense receptors respond to the same type of information. Those in your skin and ears respond to such forces as physical contact or sound waves. Receptors in your mouth and nose react to chemical substances in food and in the air.

Receptors in your eyes respond to light. Like each of the other sense organs, your eyes change the information they gather into electrical impulses. Your brain then translates the impulses into the shapes and colors of the world.

Helmet and face mask in place, a young bicycle rider adjusts his goggles before a cross-country race. This racer will use his sense of vision to find the safest, most direct route to the finish line. Dirt kicked up by speeding bikes could injure his eyes. So the racers always wear safety goggles for protection.

CHUCK O'REAR/WEST LIGHT

Bright lights of a rescue vehicle streak through the night in Seattle, Washington (opposite). The flashing lights warn motorists and pedestrians to stay clear as the vehicle races to an emergency. Your eyes bring you a constant stream of images. Some inform you. Some entertain you. Some, like this one, warn you of danger. The photographer made this unusual picture by keeping the camera shutter open while the rescue vehicle zoomed toward him. The open shutter recorded the lights as streaks on the film.

CHRIS JOHNS

Your Eyes and How They Work

Before you were born, your eyes formed as small buds attached to the front of your brain. The buds later grew into two organs that supply the brain with more information than any other sense. Your eyes are so important to your brain that about one-tenth of your cerebral cortex is devoted to vision—more than is devoted to any other sense.

For your eyes to work, they must have light. The eyes pick up light that is reflected or given off by an object. Light-sensitive receptors inside each eye change the light into nerve impulses. Your visual cortex then translates these impulses into vision.

To help you understand what you see, your brain constantly searches for patterns. Some nerve cells in the visual cortex detect the shape of an object—whether it's made up of curved or angled lines, for example. Other cells note color patterns. Your brain then tries to identify the object by comparing its shape and color with memories of things you've seen before.

Many people have compared the eye to a camera. In some ways this comparison is accurate. Like a camera, the eye has a lens. When light passes through the lens, the lens focuses it on a sensitive part of the eye called the retina (RET-nuh). The retina works somewhat like film in a camera. When light strikes the retina, a chemical reaction takes place. This reaction records the "picture" being taken by the eye.

The human eye works harder than any camera does. The eye constantly takes pictures, for an image formed on your retina quickly disappears. When you stare at an object, you may think your eyes are still. Actually, they are in slight but constant motion.

To understand how your eyes work, you need to know the parts of the eye. The painting at right shows the structures that make up the organ of sight.

The eye consists of many parts. The white of the eye is known as the sclera (SKLEHR-uh). A transparent window called the cornea (KOR-nee-uh) covers the iris—the colored part of the eye. The iris enlarges and contracts to control the amount of light passing through the pupil, a hole in the center of the iris. Just behind the iris lies the lens. This clear, flexible structure helps the eye focus, or produce a sharp image of what it sees. A jelly-like substance called the vitreous (VIH-tree-uhs) body fills the eyeball. Lining most of the inner surface of the eye is the retina. The retina contains the receptors that change light into nerve impulses. A layer of tissue called the choroid (KOHR-oyd) supports the retina by supplying it with nutrients. The optic nerve, at the back of the eye, carries nerve impulses to the visual cortex.

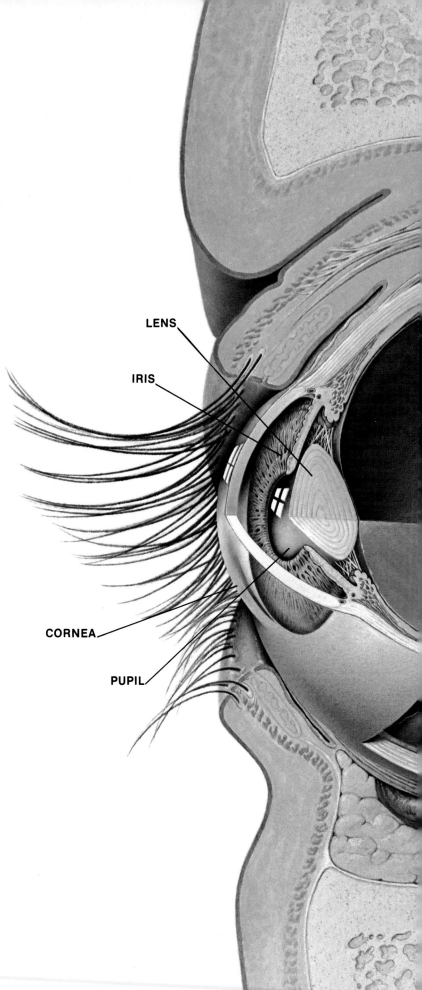

LENS

IRIS

CORNEA

PUPIL

VITREOUS BODY

OPTIC NERVE

RETINA

CHOROID

SCLERA

Judging depth and distance: When you look at an object, you see more than its shape and color. You see its thickness and how far away it is. The ability to tell these things is called depth perception. You have depth perception because your eyes are set apart in your head. Each eye sees a slightly different view of an object. The diagram below shows how some fibers from each optic nerve cross at a place called the optic chiasm (KYE-az-uhm). Nerve impulses from the right side of each eye travel to the right side of the brain. Impulses from the left side of each eye travel to the left side of the brain. Because each eye sees a slightly different picture, the visual cortex gets a "stereo" view. This enables it to interpret an object's depth and its distance from your eyes.

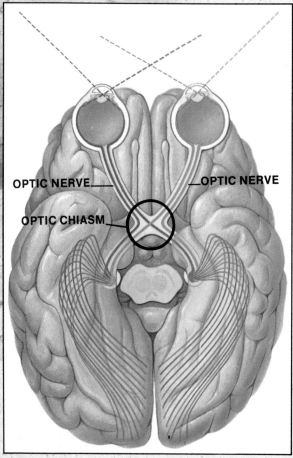

OPTIC NERVE **OPTIC NERVE**

OPTIC CHIASM

JANE HURD (BOTH)

THE IRIS GIVES THE EYE ITS COLOR AND HELPS REGULATE INCOMING LIGHT BY CHANGING THE SIZE OF THE PUPIL.

MARVIN J. FRYER

The Iris and the Pupil

When you look at a friend's eyes, you usually first notice the colored part, or iris. Your friend may have eyes that are blue, gray, green, or brown. People inherit the color of their eyes from their parents. For example, if either parent has brown eyes, the children have at least a 50 percent chance of having brown eyes, too.

A substance called melanin (MEL-uh-nuhn) gives your eyes, hair, and skin their color. The melanin colors the irises. Blue or gray eyes contain little melanin. Brown eyes contain a lot of melanin. Other colors—hazel or green, for example—contain amounts in between.

Besides giving your irises their color, melanin helps protect your eyes from bright light. People with little or no melanin in their bodies are called albinos (al-BYE-nose). These people have pale blue eyes that are very sensitive to light.

In the center of the iris is an opening called the pupil. To regulate light entering the eye, muscles in the iris adjust the size of this small round "window." In dim light, the pupil opens to let more light pass into the eye. In bright light, the pupil closes to a tiny hole to keep most of the light out. When opened wide, the pupil is l6 times larger than when it closes to its smallest point.

Open-and-shut case: The muscles of the iris adjust the size of the pupil to the level of light. In bright light, the iris makes the pupil grow small (below). Less light can then enter the eye. The transparent cornea covers the outside of the eye in front of the iris.

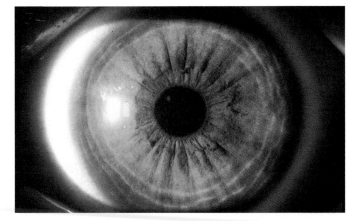

As the light grows dimmer, the iris increases the size of the pupil (below). More light can now enter the eye. The size of the pupil also increases when a person is afraid or concentrating on something. Besides controlling light, the pupil helps the eye focus on nearby objects.

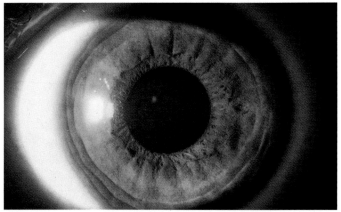

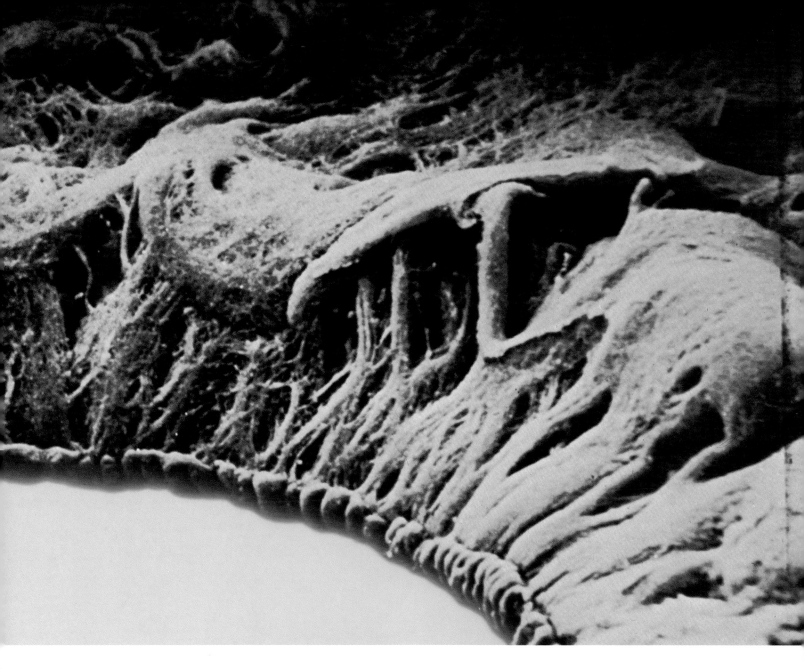

Like strands of thread around a buttonhole, muscles of the iris surround the pupil (above). The small ring of muscle just at the edge of the pupil is called the sphincter (SFINGK-ter). In bright light it pulls the iris inward, making the pupil smaller. Hidden behind the colored tissue of the iris is the dilator (die-LATE-uhr) muscle. This muscle enlarges the pupil in dim light.

Dark glasses protect the eyes of 13-year-old Wendy Falconer, of Portland, Oregon. Wendy floats in a swimming pool on a sunny day. Her sunglasses help her pupils cut down on the light entering her eyes. Wendy's eyelids also help protect her eyes. In extremely bright light, a person automatically squints. Looking at a very bright light can damage your eyes. That's why you should never look directly at the sun—not even during an eclipse, when the moon partially covers it.

DAVID FALCONER

43

Learning to Use Your Eyes

You probably opened your eyes a short time after you were born. But several weeks passed before you could see anything clearly. At first, the world appeared as a lot of fuzzy shapes. That was because your muscles hadn't strengthened enough to focus your eyes.

Your eyesight developed quickly, though. In about two months, you could focus your eyes well enough to recognize shapes and colors of objects. After about three months, you began to see with depth perception. In other words, you could use your eyes together to judge an object's thickness and its distance away. Here's what happens when you look at a distant object—a tree, for example: Your left eye and your right eye see the tree from slightly different angles. Your brain processes the images —along with what you already know about trees—in a way that enables you to judge about how far away the tree is.

Depth perception depends in part on your ability to move your eyes so they focus on an object. Six muscles control each of your eyes. These move the eyes in different directions. When you look at something far away, both of your eyes look straight ahead. When you look at closer things, your eyes turn slightly inward.

Identifying things through vision depends a lot on your memory. Each time you see an object, your brain stores its image. When you see that object again, your brain identifies it by comparing it to the previous image.

CHARLES HARBUTT/ARCHIVE

The world remains a mystery to Damian Harbutt, of New York City. Damian stares at a flower, but it's only a blur to the 6-week-old infant. Damian has not yet developed the muscle-power to focus his eyes. His eyes will begin to focus at about two months.

Russel Cummer and his pet pig see things eye to eye. Russel, 11, who lives near Sherrill, Iowa, raised the pig as a 4-H project. Although humans have better eyesight than some animals, "seeing" depends partly on understanding what you see. For example, an animal may see an object just as well as a human sees it. But if the animal's memory isn't as good as the human's, the animal may not understand or respond to what it sees.
JULIE HABEL

THE LENS CHANGES SHAPE TO
HELP THE CORNEA BRING IMAGES
INTO FOCUS.

Focusing Rays of Light

Try this simple experiment. Stretch your left arm out in front of you and hold up one finger. Hold one finger on your right hand about 6 inches (15 cm) away from your nose. Line up the two fingers. Now stare at one finger, then at the other. Do you notice anything strange happening as you look back and forth? When you stare at the near finger, the other splits into two images. But as soon as you stare at the two distant images they jump together!

This happens because your eyes can focus clearly on objects at only one distance at a time. Objects at other distances either split into double images or don't register in your brain at all. (If this experiment didn't work for you, try shifting the left finger to one side.)

Light rays coming from a distant object travel in lines that are almost parallel. The eye doesn't have to work very hard to focus these rays. In this case, the cornea does most of the work of focusing. Because of its curved shape, the cornea bends the light rays so they form a tiny image inside the eyeball. However, light rays from a nearby object tend to spread out. The eye has to work harder to focus this light. The lens must now help the cornea bend the rays. It does this by changing shape.

For example, when your eye focuses on a distant object, muscles surrounding the lens stretch it into a fairly flat shape. When you look at something nearby, the muscles allow the lens to relax into a thicker, more normal shape. Light rays passing through the cornea bend together even more as they pass through the relaxed lens.

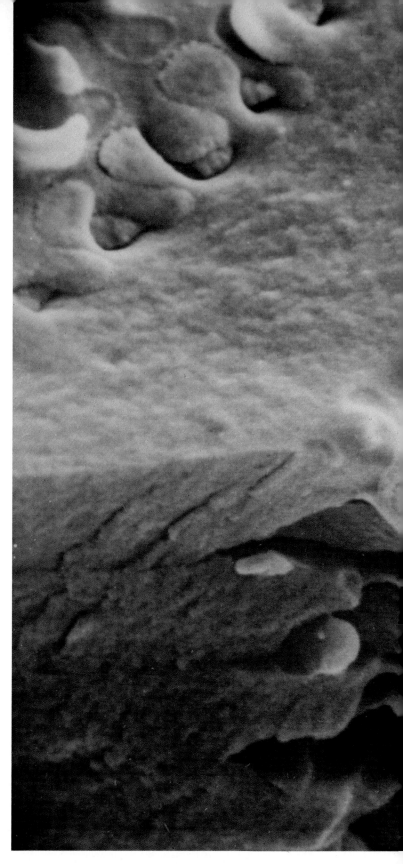

Layers of cells that form the lens of the eye look like stacks of cardboard (left). The lens grows throughout life as new cell layers build upon older ones. Older layers eventually harden. When this happens, the lens loses some of its ability to change shape. This photograph shows the lens cells magnified 810 times.

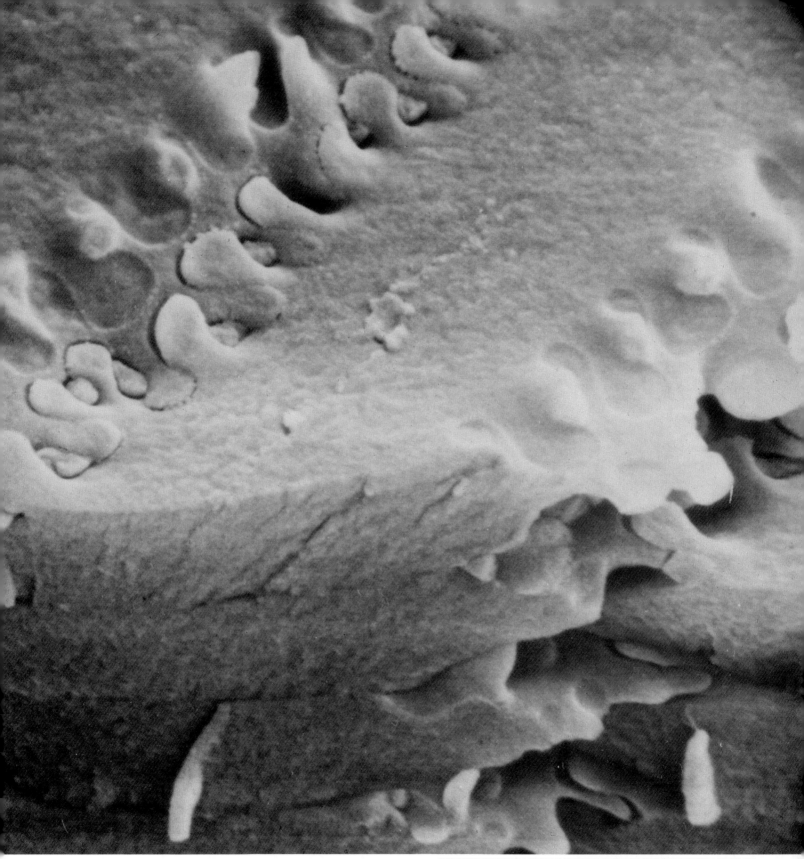

Zipperlike joints lock the cells of the lens together. The eye focuses by bending light rays into a point on the retina. By changing shape, the lens helps the eye to focus. To focus on nearby objects, the lens becomes thick and rounded. To focus on distant objects, it becomes thin and flat. This view shows the lens 6,955 times life-size.

THE RETINA CHANGES RAYS OF
LIGHT INTO NERVE IMPULSES.

Images on the Retina

A movie is playing inside your head. Together, the cornea and lens of your eye form the movie projector. The retina acts as the screen on which the cornea and lens project their images.

When you look at any object—a building or a car—the cornea and lens bend rays of light coming from the object. They focus the rays on the retina. This inner lining of the eye contains millions of receptor cells that change light rays into electrical impulses. Nerve fibers attached to the receptor cells carry the impulses to the brain. Only when the nerve impulses reach the brain do you "see" the image on the retina. In other words, vision really takes place in the brain and not in the eye.

An interesting thing happens when the cornea and lens project an image onto the retina. The image is turned upside down and reversed from left to right. The large drawing at right illustrates this. The brain interprets the image so that we see it in the correct position.

When you look at an object, your eye actually makes a series of images. Your memory briefly compares each image with the one that follows. Comparing the stream of images helps you detect motion.

Your eye can be fooled into seeing motion where there is none. This happens each time you look at an animated cartoon. The cartoon really consists of a series of individual drawings. However, the drawings flash by so quickly on the screen that your eye cannot spot the separate images. The pictures run together, creating an illusion of movement.

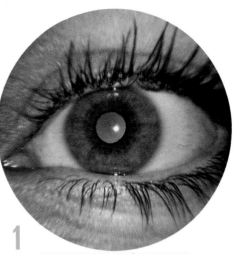

1
WILLIAM S. JOBE; DAVIS-EATON/ST. LUKE HOSPITAL
(ABOVE AND BELOW)

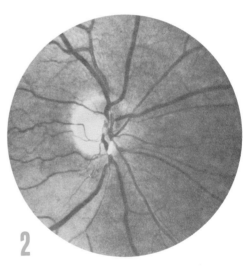

2

1 *Light passes into the eye and strikes the retina. In this picture, you can see light from a photographic flash reflecting off the retina—the orange area.*

2 *Branching blood vessels carry oxygen to all parts of the retina. Light-sensitive cells in the retina change light rays into electrical impulses. The optic nerve, the yellow area near the center, carries the impulses to your brain. Because this area contains no light-sensitive cells, it causes a tiny blind spot in your vision.*

3 *An upside-down image forms on the retina. If you could actually see such an image in someone's eye, it would look like this. The retina absorbs light rays from the image. Only when nerve impulses reach the brain do you actually see the image.*

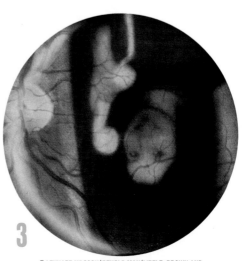

3

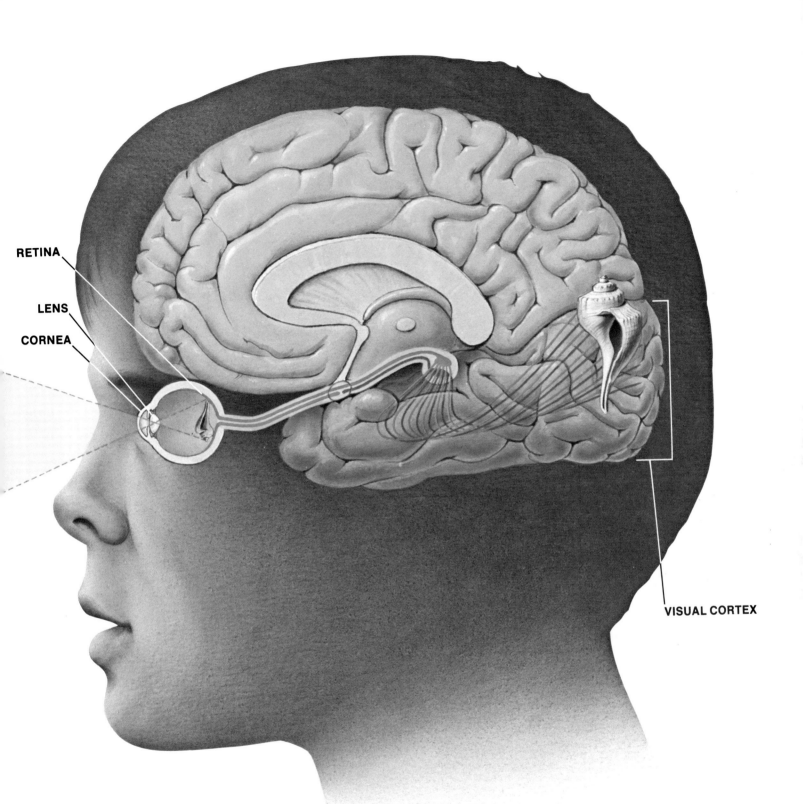

RETINA

LENS

CORNEA

VISUAL CORTEX

Did you know that you see with the back of your head? This drawing shows how the brain's visual cortex receives images detected by the eye. Light rays reflected by the seashell pass through the boy's cornea and lens. These transparent parts of the eye focus the light on the retina. Because light rays travel in straight lines, rays from the top of the seashell strike the bottom of the retina. Rays from the bottom of the shell strike the top of the retina. Therefore, they form an upside-down and reversed image. The retina's millions of nerve cells detect the light rays reflected from the shell. The cells change the rays into nerve impulses. These signals travel along a nerve pathway to the visual cortex, at the back of the head. This part of the brain begins to interpret the impulses. As it does, it switches the image of the seashell back into the correct position.

JANE HURD

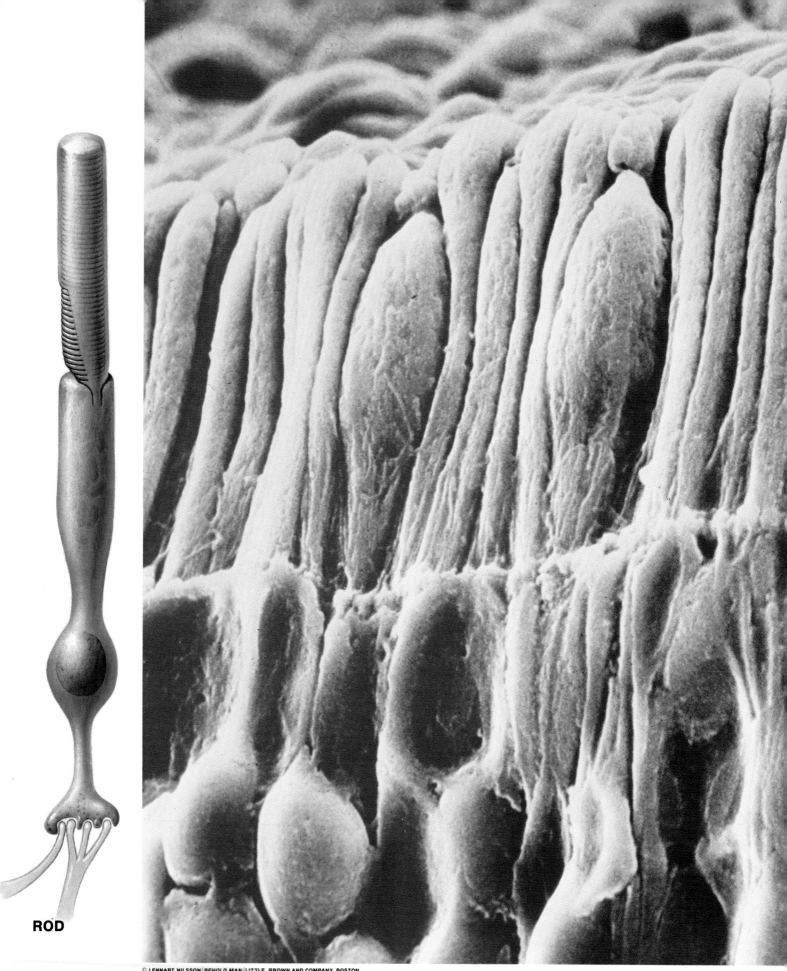

ROD

© LENNART NILSSON/*BEHOLD MAN*/LITTLE, BROWN AND COMPANY, BOSTON

Nerve Impulses in the Retina

Scientists still have a lot to discover about how the eye changes light into electrical impulses. They have learned, however, that vision depends on two kinds of light-sensitive cells. These cells are called rods and cones. They get their names from their shapes. The retina contains about 125 million rods and about 6 million cones. Rods provide vision in dim light. Cones provide vision in bright light. Cones also give you the ability to see colors.

Most of the cones lie in the center of the retina, concentrated in an area called the macula (MAC-yuh-luh). This is where your vision is sharpest. When you look directly at an object, your eye focuses the image on the macula. The center of the macula is called the fovea (FOH-vee-uh). This area gives you your best vision in bright light.

The rods lie mostly around the sides of the retina. Some cones are scattered there, too. The cells in this area enable you to see things that surround the object your eye is focusing on. The ability to see this surrounding area is called peripheral vision. It is what enables you to concentrate on one baseball player and still see the whole field.

Rods and cones both work because they contain bits of colored material called pigments. When light strikes pigments, they change shape and produce electrical activity in the receptor cells. Nerve fibers attached to the rods and cones form the optic nerve, the pathway to the brain.

All rods contain just one kind of pigment, called rhodopsin (roh-DAHP-suhn). Rhodopsin gives you visual information that your brain interprets in varying shades of gray. There are three kinds of cone cells. Each is most sensitive to blue, or green, or red light. Together, impulses from the red, green, and blue cones blend in the brain and enable you to see all the colors of the rainbow.

JANE HURD (ART)

CONE

Fat cones and skinny rods squeeze together in the retina. More than 130 million of these light-sensitive cells line the retina. Rods produce vision in shades of gray. Cones produce vision in colors. When light strikes material called pigments in the rods and cones, the rods and cones create nerve impulses. The drawing at left shows a single cone. The drawing opposite shows an individual rod. Part of each has been peeled back to show the stacks of disks that contain pigments. Nerve fibers, shown in yellow, extend from the bases of the rod and the cone. These fibers connect with other nerve fibers that carry impulses to the visual cortex.

Children boarding a bus in early morning see a world of gray. Only the sun and the lights of the bus provide enough light to produce color. All other colors fade to shades of gray in the dim light. Cones, the cells of the retina that detect color, work only in bright light. The cells called rods provide vision in low light. But rods can only detect objects as patterns of light and dark. Without color, the eye has a difficult time placing an object in relation to its background. Because of this, the eye's ability to judge distances is not good at night. Since it cannot tell distances as well, the eye also has a more difficult job focusing in the dark.

Although the cones in your retina provide sharp vision during the day, they do not work well in dim light. That is the reason colored things look gray in the dark. At night, your rods take over the job of providing vision. Because the rods lie mostly at the edges of the retina, you can sometimes see an object better in the dark by not looking directly at it. Sailors learned this long ago. When sailors stand watch at night, they look for the lights of other ships. But they don't look along the horizon. Instead, they look just above the line where the ocean and the sky meet. That way, if they see a light, it will fall on the sides of their retina—where the rods can detect it.

In very bright light, however, a rod temporarily loses the pigment it contains and cannot create an electrical impulse. The rod must renew the pigment before it can send another impulse. Pigments in the rods build up again mostly in the dark. It can take half an hour or longer for the pigments to return to normal. That is why you have a hard time seeing when you first enter a darkened movie house from a brightly lit lobby.

One part of the retina has no rods or cones. This is the area near the center of the retina where nerve fibers gather to form the optic nerve. Because this area cannot respond to light, it is called the blind spot.

You seldom notice that your eye has a blind spot, however. Your eye moves so often that this small spot doesn't stay fixed on the same area very long. Also, the blind spot lies in a different area of each retina, so that whatever one eye cannot detect the other eye can.

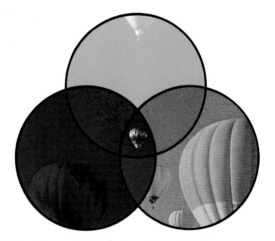

Hot-air balloons fill the sky above Albuquerque, New Mexico (opposite). Bright sunlight brings out their many colors. The retina's cone cells are primarily sensitive to three kinds of light—red, green, and blue. Your brain mixes these colors to create others. In all, humans can recognize more than 200 colors. The three circles above show how the brain creates all the colors you can see from red, green, and blue. The left circle shows part of the photograph at right as detected by red-sensitive cones. The circle at right shows how the photograph appears to green-sensitive cones. The top circle shows how blue-sensitive cones see the photograph. Other colors result when the brain mixes the nerve signals sent out by the red, green, and blue cone cells. Where the three colors combine, in the center, all the colors of the original photograph result.

Problems Seeing Color

Some people think the ocean is blue, but it isn't. If you've seen the ocean on a cloudy day, you know it sometimes looks green. However, the ocean isn't green either. In fact, it isn't any color at all—and neither is anything else.

Objects themselves do not actually have color. Color is simply a sensation in your brain caused by the light coming from an object. Your brain interprets different kinds of light as different colors. The brains of most people interpret light in the same way. We agree that the sky is blue. We say that grass is green. However, some people have trouble telling one color from another. These people are color-blind.

People with color blindness may have problems with the cones in their retina, or there may be something wrong with the nerve pathway connecting their eyes and brain.

Scientists have learned that about eight out of a hundred males are color-blind to some extent. One female in a hundred has difficulty with color vision. Although color blindness cannot be corrected, it doesn't get worse.

SUSAN T. MCELHINNEY (PHOTOGRAPHS)

Problems Seeing Near or Far

As the painting on pages 40-41 shows, a normal eyeball has an almost perfectly round shape. For a person to see clearly, the cornea and lens must focus light rays entering the eye. The cornea and lens do this by bending the rays that come from one point of an object until they come to a point on the retina.

But not everyone is born with perfectly shaped eyeballs. Some eyeballs are too long from front to back. Others are too short. In both these cases, the cornea and lens cannot bring rays of light together so they focus on the retina.

People whose eyeballs are too long are said to be nearsighted. These people can usually see nearby objects clearly, but they have trouble seeing distant objects. Because their eyeballs are too long, rays of light from distant objects come into focus in front of their retinas.

The opposite of nearsightedness is farsightedness. This problem occurs when the eyeballs are too short from front to back. A farsighted person can usually see faraway objects clearly, but nearby objects look blurry. Since a farsighted eyeball is shorter than normal, light rays from nearby objects come into focus behind the retina. Most people with either of these two problems can see normally with corrective glasses.

NORMAL VISION *Andrea Parker, 16, floats in a neighbor's pool in Arlington, Virginia. To a person with normal vision, both the boat in front of Andrea and the flowerpots behind her would look clear and sharp. As the diagram at right shows, rays of light come to a point on the retina of a normal eye. When this occurs, both nearby and faraway objects appear in focus.*

Roses are red, violets are blue—or are they? Some people cannot tell one color from another. These people are color-blind. In the most common kind of color blindness, the person cannot tell red from green. The colored dots at left contain an image. If you have normal color vision, you will see a blue-green bird in the center. If you have red-green color blindness, you will see only pink and yellow dots. Color vision depends on the red, green, and blue cones of the retina. Color blindness results if something is wrong with some of the cones or with the nerves that carry their signals to the brain. Even if you can't see a bird among the dots, you may not have a vision problem. But only an eye doctor can tell for sure.

MARVIN J. FRYER (ABOVE AND ART BELOW)

NEARSIGHTED VISION *To a nearsighted person, Andrea and the flowers behind her appear as a blur. The boat, however, appears clear. The diagram at right shows that a nearsighted eye is longer than* 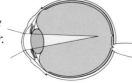 *normal. Light rays from distant objects meet in front of the retina. When the image reaches the retina, the rays are spreading out and the image is blurred.*

FARSIGHTED VISION *A farsighted person would still see Andrea as a blur. The toy boat also would look out of focus, but the flowers would be distinct. As the diagram shows, a farsighted eye is* 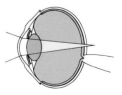 *shorter than normal. Light rays from nearby objects come into focus behind the retina and nearby objects are blurred. Only faraway objects are clearly seen.*

55

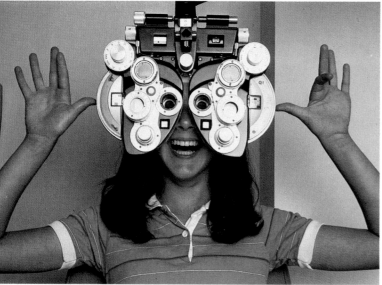

Andrea Parker discovers that an eye examination can be fun. Andrea sits behind a Phoropter (fuh-ROP-ter)—a machine used to test her vision. Having your eyes checked regularly is important. During the first 12 years of life, most learning takes place through vision. Many children don't do well in school simply because they cannot see well. For some children, eyeglasses improve the ability to read and to learn.

A pinpoint of light burns away a diseased blood vessel inside a man's eye. The light is called a laser beam. It passes through the front of the eye without causing damage. A doctor aims the beam at blood vessels in the patient's retina. The light destroys the diseased vessels, improving the man's vision. Doctors use laser beams to treat many eye problems. Previously, they could only operate on the eye by hand. Laser beams have made certain eye operations safer and less painful.

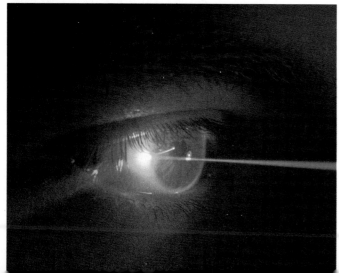

Taking Care of Your Eyes

You probably know already that it's easier to take good care of something than to repair it after it's damaged. That's especially true of your eyes. Your eyes are so important that you should do everything you can to take care of them. The most important thing you can do for your eyes is to have them examined regularly.

Doctors recommend that parents have a baby's eyes checked shortly after the baby is born. Each person should have a checkup every few years up to the age of 40. After that, a person should have an annual eye examination. Even if you have good vision, you should still see an eye doctor from time to time. Doctors can detect certain diseases in other parts of the body just by checking a person's eyes.

You should also have your eyes examined anytime you have problems. Common eye problems include blurry vision, pain in the eyes, squinting, or frequent headaches. You should immediately see a doctor if you get a sharp object in your eyes, such as a piece of metal or glass. If you ever get a chemical splashed in your eyes, rinse them with water for several minutes. Then call a doctor right away.

When you have your eyes checked, your doctor may recommend eyeglasses. People have worn glasses for a long time. The Chinese invented them about 700 years ago. Benjamin Franklin invented bifocals—glasses for both near and far vision—in 1784. Today, about half the people in the United States wear eyeglasses or contact lenses.

Some people prefer to wear contact lenses instead of eyeglasses. Many people feel that they look better with contacts. Active people, such as athletes, prefer contacts because they don't get in the way as much as eyeglasses do. Your doctor may say that contacts are right for you. If so, be sure to follow the doctor's advice on how to wear them. For example, never moisten contacts by placing them in your mouth. You can get an eye infection that way.

Whether you wear eyeglasses or not, be sure to protect your eyes from bright lights and from flying objects. Sunglasses can help guard your eyes from harsh lights. Goggles can keep flying objects out of your eyes. Always remember, protecting your eyes increases the chances that they will serve you well for the rest of your life.

Visitor from another planet? No. This girl is having her new contact lenses checked to see if they fit. The girl's face appears blue because her doctor has aimed a special light at her eyes. Dye placed in the girl's eyes makes her contacts show up as green. If too much green shows, the doctor knows the contacts are too loose. Too little green means the contacts are too tight. Contact lenses must fit the eye exactly in order to work, and to feel comfortable.

4

Taste and Smell

Vision may be the sense that provides the most information about what is happening around you. But the senses of taste and smell help you almost as much as vision does. Together, taste and smell make a necessary process—eating—also an enjoyable one.

Taste and smell are both called chemical senses. That's because the sense receptors in your mouth and nose respond to chemical substances. Taste receptors respond to chemical substances that are found naturally in food or drink. Smell receptors respond to chemical substances in the air. The substances cause these receptors to send out nerve impulses that the brain interprets as taste and smell.

When you eat, your brain combines sensations of smell with those of taste. This enables you to experience many flavors. In fact, if you can't smell the food you're eating, it has little taste. For example, if you close your eyes and hold your nose shut, you may not be able to tell the difference between the taste of an apple and that of a turnip.

Besides giving you pleasure when you eat, taste and smell help protect you from harmful substances. Many poisons taste harsh or bitter. Your sense of taste warns you not to eat these substances. And your sense of smell protects you by detecting spoiled food or dangerous gases.

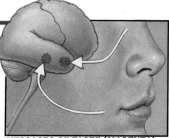

MESSAGES OF TASTE (MAGENTA) AND SMELL (PURPLE) TRAVEL BY SEPARATE PATHWAYS TO DIFFERENT AREAS OF THE BRAIN. TASTE MESSAGES GO TO THE GUSTATORY (GUSS-tuh-toh-ree) CORTEX; SMELL MESSAGES TO TO THE OLFACTORY (AHL-FAK-toh-ree) CORTEX. THE BRAIN COMBINES THESE MESSAGES TO ENABLE YOU TO EXPERIENCE THE MANY FLAVORS OF THE FOODS YOU EAT.

Scientist Peter B. Johnsen studies fish called tilapia (tuh-LAHP-ee-uh). Tilapia are often raised for food. Dr. Johnsen wants to find out how these fish decide which plants to eat. He hopes to discover a way to increase the appetites of fish used for food. This would cause the fish to grow faster and help increase the world's food supply. Dr. Johnsen works at the Monell Chemical Senses Center, in Philadelphia, Pennsylvania. Studies such as his may also help us learn more about why humans prefer certain tastes.

NICK KELSH

Pucker power: Audrey Lowndes makes a face as she tastes a sour lemon (left). Humans can detect four basic tastes. Scientists generally classify them as sweet, sour, salty, and bitter. Different flavors result when the brain combines these four tastes with sensations of smell. People without a sense of smell can detect only the four basic tastes. Doctors sometimes discover that patients who complain that nothing tastes right to them actually have a problem with their sense of smell.

NATIONAL GEOGRAPHIC SOCIETY PHOTOGRAPHER JOSEPH H. BAILEY

The Tongue's Job in Tasting

You may not realize it, but your tongue is very talented. For one thing, this flexible muscle inside your mouth helps you form words when you speak. The tongue's other important job is to detect the tastes of things you eat and drink. Your tongue detects tastes through tiny organs called taste buds. A taste bud looks somewhat like a navel orange. It is actually a cluster of taste receptor cells. Taste buds line the tongue and other parts of the mouth, but most taste buds are located on the tongue. There are several thousand taste buds on the tongue of an adult, and each taste bud may contain as many as 50 receptor cells.

Taste buds cluster together in structures that stick up from the surface of the tongue. These structures are called papillae (puh-PILL-ee). If you look at your tongue in a mirror, you can see some of them. The papillae give your tongue its rough appearance.

Each taste bud has a small pore, or opening, on its outer surface. Dissolved particles of food or drink enter the taste bud through this opening. The particles cause the receptor cells inside the taste bud to send nerve impulses to the brain. Various kinds of food cause the receptor cells to send out different messages. No one knows exactly how this happens. But somehow the brain interprets the messages as different tastes. Your brain also receives information about things you eat or drink from other sense receptors inside your mouth. These tell your brain if something is hot or cold. They also provide information about how the food feels—whether it's creamy or stringy, for example.

Other sense organs supply additional information. Your eyes tell you whether something looks good to eat. Your ears pick up sounds while you are eating—the crunch of celery or the snap of a cracker. Your brain studies these signals along with those provided by your tongue and your sense of smell. The brain puts all the signals together to give you a complete experience of the things you eat.

Thick and thin papillae poke up from the surface of the tongue (right). The thick, rounded structures are known as fungiform (FUN-juh-form) papillae. They contain from one to five taste buds, the organs of taste. Chemicals in food or drink cause the taste buds to signal the brain. The brain identifies the signals as different tastes. Other kinds of papillae may have thousands of taste buds. In all, the tongue of the average adult contains several thousand taste buds. Because of taste buds, you are able to tell if a substance is sweet, sour, salty, or bitter.

*Double-duty muscle: The tongue helps you to speak and to taste what you eat or drink. The tongue is attached to the bottom and back of the mouth. There, a movable flap called the epiglottis (ep-uh-*GLAHT*-us) keeps food from entering the lungs when you swallow. Four kinds of tiny structures called papillae cover the tongue. Fungiform and filiform (*FILL*-uh-form) papillae cover the front half. Foliate (*FOH*-lee-uht) and vallate (*VAL*-ate) papillae cover the back of the tongue. In addition to taste receptors, the tongue contains receptors that detect pressure and temperature. These send information to the brain about the texture and temperature of things you eat and drink. The brain combines this information with sensations from the taste buds.*

MARVIN J. FRYER

The Sensations of Taste

Why does the tongue detect sweet, sour, salty, and bitter tastes? No one really knows. But some scientists think the ability to tell tastes apart may be important for survival.

The ability to detect sweet and bitter tastes, for example, could have been important to our ancestors. When humans searched for food long ago, they probably relied on their sense of taste to help them tell the difference between good foods and harmful substances. People quickly learned that most sweet foods could be eaten safely and that many bitter tasting things were poisonous.

Scientists have discovered that from birth humans crave sweet tastes. On the other hand, people have a natural dislike for bitter flavors. Your taste buds cannot always tell you whether a substance is good or bad, however. Some poisons actually taste sweet, and not all bitter tastes are harmful.

Many scientists now believe that any taste bud is able to detect all of the basic tastes. However, some taste buds are more sensitive to one taste than to others. For example, taste buds at the back of the tongue are more sensitive to bitter tastes.

Often, different people react to the same tastes in different ways—usually out of habit or from past experience. Many people, for example, form the habit of adding a lot of salt to their food. Other people sometimes avoid foods that make them think of an unpleasant experience—an upset stomach, perhaps.

Cultural habits help a person learn to like or dislike certain tastes. People who depend on the sea for food often consider such things as squids and raw fish to be delicacies. People of other cultures eat foods so spicy that one bite might send you running for a glass of water. People unfamiliar with such foods might consider them distasteful.

Taste bud in action: Chemicals from food or drink enter a taste bud through a small opening on the surface of the tongue. Only liquids can pass through the opening. Saliva in your mouth helps dissolve solid foods. Each taste bud contains as many as 50 receptor cells. Chemicals entering the taste bud cause the receptor cells to release chemical transmitters. When the transmitters reach the taste nerve, at the base of the taste bud, the nerve fires electrical impulses that travel to the brain. In the cerebral cortex, they are interpreted as tastes.

MARVIN J. FRYER/BASED ON WILLIAMS, P. L., AND WARWICK, R. (1980), *GRAY'S ANATOMY*, 36TH EDITION, EDINBURGH, CHURCHILL LIVINGSTONE

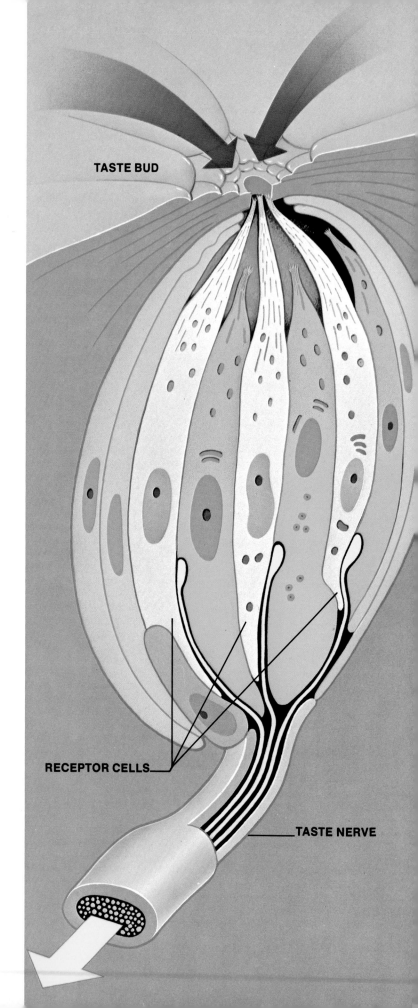

TASTE BUD

RECEPTOR CELLS

TASTE NERVE

Lemon juice sucked through a peppermint stick creates an unexpected taste sensation for Charles Muse (right). Memories of things you've tasted before can influence your reaction to food. You sometimes expect things to taste different from the way they do. Charles knows that a lemon tastes sour and that peppermint candy tastes sweet. However, he is not sure what to expect when the two tastes are mixed. Charles's taste buds sense both sweet and sour. But his brain is confused because it associates separate memories of "lemon" and "peppermint" with the combination he tastes now.

Youngsters enjoy the sweet tastes of watermelon and cantaloupe (below). From the left, they are Jenny Jasper, 11; Tom Jasper, 4; and Tammy Maiers, 9. All three live in Holy Cross, Iowa. Humans like sweet tastes from the moment they are born. Some animals, such as horses and dogs, like sweets, too. However, if you try to bribe a cat with something sweet, you're wasting your time. Cats don't respond to sweet flavors.

SUSAN T. MCELHINNEY

JULIE HABEL

Yuk! Thomas Parker, 12, of Arlington, Virginia, reacts to the taste of strong coffee (below). Coffee contains caffeine, a bitter-tasting substance. Because humans have a natural dislike for bitter flavors, most people do not care for the taste of coffee when they first try it. But many people learn to like coffee. This is known as acquiring a taste. You often acquire a taste for foods you do not like at first. For example, children usually do not care for such things as mustard or ginger, but most older people enjoy these tastes.

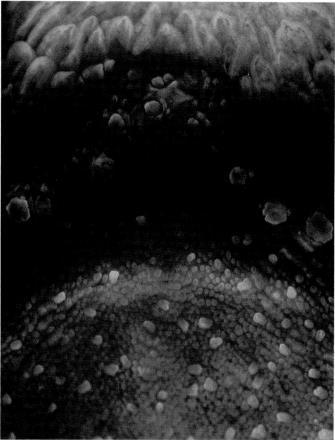

Line of defense: A V-shaped pattern of papillae at the back of the tongue (above) may help protect you from poisons. The taste buds in these papillae are sensitive to bitter tastes. When the taste buds detect a very bitter substance, they trigger an automatic response called the "gag reflex." This causes you to spit out the bitter substance. Even newborn babies have this reflex. Taste buds that detect bitter flavors are also sensitive to other tastes. Scientists have not discovered any important differences in structure among taste buds. Some are simply more sensitive to certain tastes than to others.

Lisa Stokes tastes grains of table salt with the tip of her tongue (right). Dry foods such as salt have no taste until they dissolve. Saliva on Lisa's tongue quickly dissolves the salt grains. Humans require a certain amount of salt in their diet. Animals also require salt. That's why plant-eating animals such as deer search for deposits of salt to lick. Taste receptor cells in your tongue and mouth are continually being replaced. An individual receptor cell lives only for about eight days. After that, a new cell replaces it. This is your body's way of keeping your taste buds working.

Detecting Odors in the Air

If you thought your nose was only good for smelling flowers and for giving you a preview of tonight's dinner, think of this: There are people who use their noses every day to help protect you from illness. Thomas Weber, of Brooklyn, New York, is one of them. An employee of the federal government, Weber inspects food by smelling it.

As part of his job, Weber sniffs shipments of fish to see if any part of a shipment has spoiled. Fish that fail to pass this inspection cannot be sold to the public. You might wonder why the government doesn't use machines to sort out the spoiled fish. The reason is simple. No machine ever built is as sensitive to smells as the human nose.

In fact, the human nose is so sensitive to some substances—the odor of a skunk, for example—that it can pick out just a trace of it in the air. Scientists have even found that humans can smell certain odors that cannot be detected at all by laboratory equipment.

However, even though your sense of smell is very keen, it is not nearly so effective as that of some animals. Bloodhounds can trail a person just by following the person's scent left behind on the ground. Certain kinds of male moths can smell a female moth from several miles away.

You aren't able to detect odors as well as many animals can because you do not depend on smell as much as they do. Instead, you rely more on vision and hearing to help you find out what is happening around you. But smell is still very important to humans.

Like your sense of taste, your sense of smell responds to chemical substances. When you breathe, the substances in the air stimulate receptor cells inside your nose. The receptor cells send out messages that the brain interprets as smell. The receptor cells are located in two patches of tissue called the olfactory epithelium (ahl-FAK-tuh-ree ep-uh-THEE-lee-uhm). This material lines the upper part of each nasal passage—just above and behind the bridge of your nose. Each patch is about the size of a dime, and each one contains about five million receptor cells.

Mucus (MYEW-kus), a thick fluid that keeps tissue moist, covers the olfactory epithelium. Cilia (SILL-ee-uh)—tiny hairs—on the ends of the receptor cells extend down into this layer of mucus. The mucus absorbs vaporized substances in the air you breathe, and the substances stimulate the cilia. This causes the receptor cells to send nerve impulses to the brain.

(Continued on page 68)

Jodi Rathbun, 9, of West Stockbridge, Massachusetts, sniffs a spring flower. Jodi detects the scent of the blossom with smell receptors located deep inside her nose. The drawing above shows the position of the receptors. They lie at the upper end of the nasal passages, behind the bridge of your nose. Chemical substances in the flower's fragrance cause the receptors to send impulses to the brain. The brain interprets the impulses as smells. Smell receptors cannot detect a substance unless it has vaporized. Some solid substances do not vaporize—and so have no odor.

DAN MCCOY/RAINBOW; JANE HURD

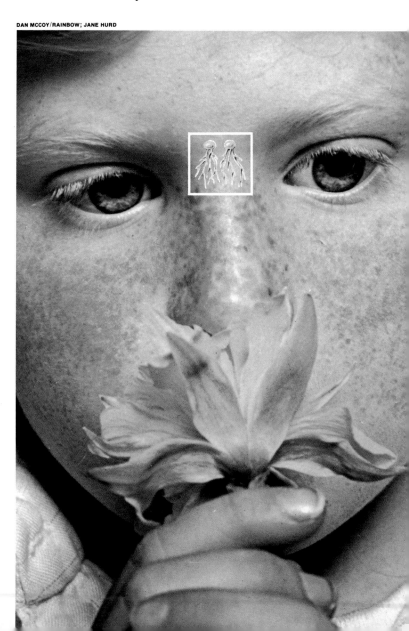

OLFACTORY BULB

OLFACTORY TRACT

RECEPTOR CELLS WITH CILIA

OLFACTORY EPITHELIUM

NASAL PASSAGE

Messages of smell reach the brain through the nose. Lining the roof of each nasal passage is a small patch of tissue called the olfactory epithelium. This soft tissue contains millions of smell receptor cells, or olfactory neurons. A layer of thick fluid called mucus keeps this tissue moist. Cilia—tiny hairs—on the ends of the receptor cells extend from the olfactory epithelium into the layer of mucus. When air passes over the mucus, the mucus absorbs vaporized substances from the air. The substances lock into receptor sites on the cilia. This causes the receptor cells to create nerve impulses. Nerves carry the impulses through a thin layer of bone to the olfactory bulb, one of a pair of smell relay stations. These communicate with the brain by a nerve pathway known as the olfactory tract. Messages of smell travel along this nerve pathway to the parts of the brain that interpret them.

JANE HURD

(Continued from page 66)

No one knows just how the dissolved substances act on the cilia. And no one has discovered how the receptor cells recognize various odors. But somehow the brain sorts out and interprets the signals sent out by receptor cells. As a result, you can tell the difference between thousands of different smells.

Nerve impulses from the smell receptors travel to a pair of relay stations known as the olfactory bulbs. These structures send the messages of smell directly to the areas of the brain that can further interpret such signals.

The messages first pass through a part of the brain called the limbic system, an area associated with your memories and emotions. This may explain why odors often bring back vivid memories. For example, the smell of burning wood may suddenly make you think of the first time you went camping.

In addition to smell receptors, your nose, mouth, and tongue contain a network of nerves that form the trigeminal (try-JEM-uh-nuhl) system. The body reacts with pain when these nerves are exposed to irritants, such as ammonia or vinegar. The trigeminal system can protect you by warning you about harmful chemicals in the air.

Scientists have discovered that people are not born with any preferences for odors. You learn to like certain smells through experience. Some people actually like odors that others think are terrible. Reseachers have also learned that people temporarily get used to smells. If that weren't true, no one would want to work as a chemist for a living.

Brad Wolter, 13, of Holy Cross, Iowa, holds his nose to keep from smelling a pile of garbage (below). Holding your nose blocks off smells by keeping air from reaching the receptor cells of the olfactory epithelium. Smell receptor cells temporarily get used to odors. If Brad didn't hold his nose, he would eventually no longer notice the smell of the garbage. Unpleasant odors can actually be useful. For example, gas companies add a strong scent to natural gas, which is otherwise odorless. The added scent enables people to notice dangerous gas leaks.

JULIE HABEL

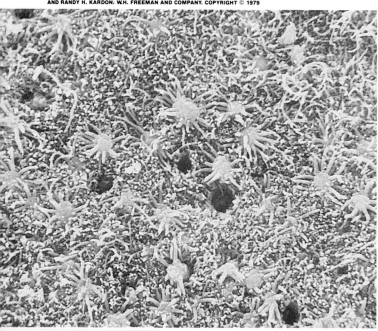

Close-up of the olfactory epithelium (left) shows the cilia that react to odors. Each receptor cell has as many as 150 cilia extending from its tip. The length and thickness of the cilia vary. The tips of some receptors stick up farther than others. These are the large, spider-shaped structures you see here. Some of the dark holes are the openings of Bowman's glands. These structures produce mucus. Other holes contain receptors that lie deeper in the epithelium.

Smell detectors at work: Air passes across the mucus-covered surface of the olfactory epithelium (right). Vaporized substances in the air bind with the tiny hairs, or cilia, at the ends of receptor cells. Nerve fibers extend from the opposite ends of the cells. Bundles of these fibers carry nerve impulses to the olfactory bulbs, where the messages of smell are passed on to the brain. Besides receptor cells, the olfactory epithelium contains cells that help support the receptors. It also contains Bowman's glands.

OLFACTORY EPITHELIUM

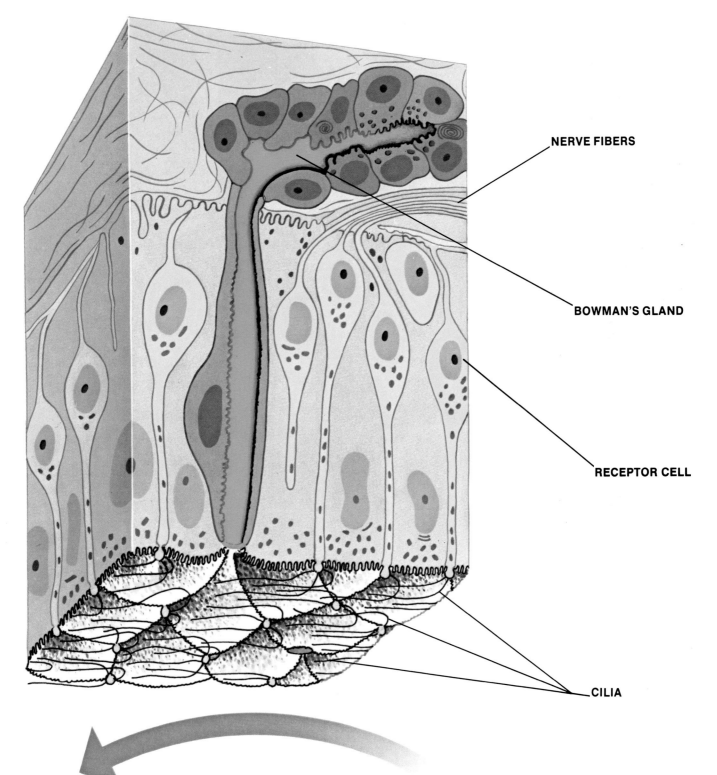

NERVE FIBERS

BOWMAN'S GLAND

RECEPTOR CELL

CILIA

MARVIN J. FRYER/BASED ON WILLIAMS, P. L., AND WARWICK, R. (1980), *GRAY'S ANATOMY,* 36TH EDITION,
EDINBURGH, CHURCHILL LIVINGSTONE

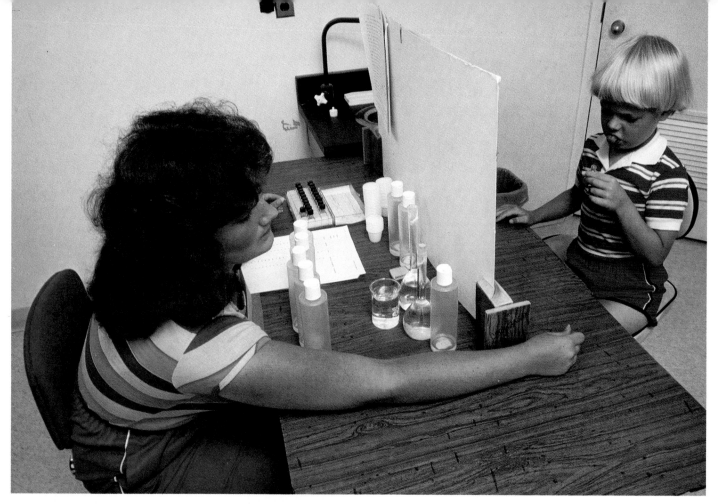

An unpleasant odor makes Raymond Beauchamp stick out his tongue (above). Raymond, 5, of Philadephia, Pennsylvania, is taking a test to see if he can smell a variety of odors. Elizabeth Konowal, a researcher at the Monell Chemical Senses Center, will then find out the smallest amounts of certain odors that Raymond can detect. Such tests have revealed no differences between children and adults in the ability to detect various odors. Scientists hope to find an odor that will keep children away from poisons. With practice, humans can learn to recognize several thousand odors. Researchers have found that people often recognize an odor but are unable to identify it by name. Although their noses are working fine, their brains simply cannot come up with a label for the smell.

Raymond squints as he takes a whiff of ammonia. Harsh-smelling chemicals such as ammonia stimulate trigeminal nerves inside the nose. Such nerves react with messages of pain. The brain combines the trigeminal signals with those of smell to help identify some odors. The powerful smell of ammonia makes Raymond's nose run. Glands inside his nose have released fluids to get rid of the irritating substance.

How does the nose distinguish different odors? Scientists aren't sure, but they have come up with several ideas. They do know that many substances give off vapor made up of molecules (MAHL-ih-kyewls), groups of tiny particles. Molecules of each substance have a distinctive shape. These molecules may stimulate olfactory nerve cells by fitting into similarly shaped openings called receptor sites. The sites are found on the cilia. Each molecule fits into a certain receptor site much the way a key fits into a lock. When a molecule has filled a receptor site, the nerve cell sends impulses to the olfactory bulb. Some scientists think that the brain identifies different odors by interpreting which receptor sites have been filled. But the scientists don't yet understand all the details of how this happens. They point out that molecules with the same shape don't always smell the same. And some molecules with different shapes do smell alike. The pictures below show, in a simplified way, how the molecule-receptor theory might work.

Peppermint

PEPPERMINT SMELLS MINTY. THE DRAWING AT LEFT SHOWS THE MOLECULE THAT MAKES UP A MINTY ODOR, ALONG WITH THE RECEPTOR SITE THAT IT MIGHT FIT. BOTH HAVE A GENERALLY OVAL SHAPE.

Lemon

A LEMON SMELLS PUNGENT, OR SHARP. THE DRAWING AT LEFT SHOWS A MOLECULE OF A SHARP ODOR AND THE RECEPTOR SITE INTO WHICH IT MIGHT FIT. BOTH THE MOLECULE AND THE RECEPTOR SITE HAVE GENERALLY SPHERICAL—ROUND—SHAPES.

Floral

THE FRAGRANCE OF A ROSE IS AN EXAMPLE OF A FLORAL SMELL. THE DRAWING AT LEFT SHOWS A MOLECULE FROM A FLORAL ODOR, WHICH HAS AN IRREGULAR SHAPE. THE POSSIBLE RECEPTOR SITE FOR THIS MOLECULE, BELOW IT, ALSO HAS AN IRREGULAR SHAPE.

MARVIN J. FRYER/ADAPTED FROM: *ATLAS OF THE BODY AND MIND.* COPYRIGHT MITCHELL BEAZLEY PUBLISHERS, LTD. 1976. PUBLISHED IN THE U.S. BY RAND MCNALLY & COMPANY AND ALSO ADAPTED FROM: *THE STEREOCHEMICAL THEORY OF ODOR,* J. E. AMOORE, J. W. JOHNSTON, JR., AND M. RUBIN, SCIENTIFIC AMERICAN

5

Hearing and Balance

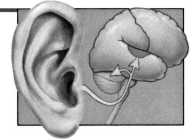

Think back to the last time you went to a parade. Remember how many different sounds you heard? As marching bands went by, sounds poured in from every direction. Drums boomed. Trumpets blared. Whistles tweeted.

Your ears bring you just as many sounds on a quiet country lane. They bring you the gentle rustle of the leaves. Twigs snap underfoot as you walk. You hear the sounds of birds chirping and insects buzzing.

Without your ears, you couldn't hear one of the most important sounds in the world—the human voice. Hearing helps you communicate with others through speech.

You hear because your ears are able to detect sound waves in the air. When things move, they cause the air to vibrate, or move back and forth. When you clap your hands, for example, you create vibrations. These travel outward in waves, like ripples spreading in water. Your ears detect these sound waves and change them into nerve impulses. The impulses travel along nerve pathways to the brain. There they are interpreted as sounds.

Your ears do another important job, too. They help you keep your balance. A part of the ear detects movements by your head in any direction. Signals from this part of the ear help your brain control the muscles needed to keep your body steady.

1 *You begin to hear sounds when vibrating air strikes the eardrum, a tightly stretched membrane, or thin layer of tissue. A tiny bone called the hammer is attached to the eardrum. This picture shows the eardrum and hammer from inside the head.*

2 *Sound waves make the eardrum vibrate. The hammer moves back and forth each time the eardrum moves. In this way the hammer helps pass the vibrations on to other parts of the ear, where they are changed into nerve impulses. The movement of the eardrum in this photograph has been exaggerated. Sound waves cause such slight vibrations in the eardrum that you could not actually see it move.*

© LENNART NILSSON/*BEHOLD MAN*/LITTLE, BROWN AND COMPANY, BOSTON (BOTH)

Sounds of fifes lead marchers in a parade in Basel, Switzerland (left). The marchers are taking part in the Basel Carnival. During this three-day celebration, both children and adults dress in bright costumes, put on masks, and parade through the streets. Music is an important part of the carnival, held each year in February or March. Residents hope that fifes and drums will help drive away winter. Music demonstrates the wide range of sounds your ears can detect—from the high tweet of fifes to the deep boom of drums.

JOSEPH F. VIESTI

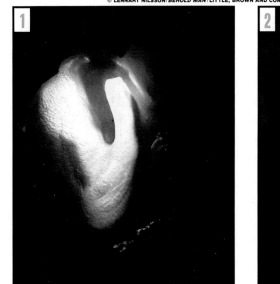

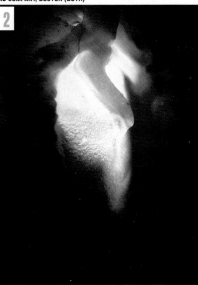

Your Ears and How They Work

You may have thought your ears were those two flexible flaps on the sides of your head. Actually, the flaps are only part of your ears. The entire ear extends deep inside your skull. It has three main parts: the outer ear, the middle ear, and the inner ear. The outer ear's job is to gather sound waves and direct them to the middle ear. The middle ear amplifies the sound waves—increases their force—and passes them on to the inner ear. There the waves are changed into nerve impulses. The brain then interprets the impulses as sounds.

The outer ear begins with the flap of skin on the side of the head, which most people call the ear. Its technical name is the auricle (AWR-ih-kuhl). The auricle funnels sound waves into the auditory canal, the small opening in the ear. This canal—about an inch (2½ cm) long, leads inside your head to the eardrum.

The eardrum, a thin, almost circular membrane at the end of the auditory canal, completes the outer ear. When sound waves strike the eardrum, it vibrates.

Inside the middle ear are three connected bones, the hammer, the anvil, and the stirrup. The hammer is attached to the inside of the eardrum. Sound waves that make the eardrum vibrate also cause the hammer to move. The hammer's motion causes the other two bones to vibrate. The stirrup relays the vibrations of the hammer to the inner ear through an opening called the oval window. The stirrup's vibrations cause fluid in a chamber called the cochlea (KO-klee-uh) to vibrate. Hair cells inside the cochlea change the vibrations of the fluid into nerve impulses that travel to the brain.

The inner ear also contains three organs of balance—the utricle (YEW-trih-kuhl), the saccule (SACK-yewl), and the semicircular canals.

AURICLE

Sean Bland, 11, plays a waltz in his violin class in Birmingham, Alabama (left). The drawing on Sean's face shows the location of the ear structures. The ear begins with the fleshy flap on the outside of the head and extends far into the skull. The organ of hearing lies below and behind the eye. Sean is learning to play the violin by listening to recorded music. On his own violin, he imitates the music he has heard.

MIKE CLEMMER/MARVIN J. FRYER

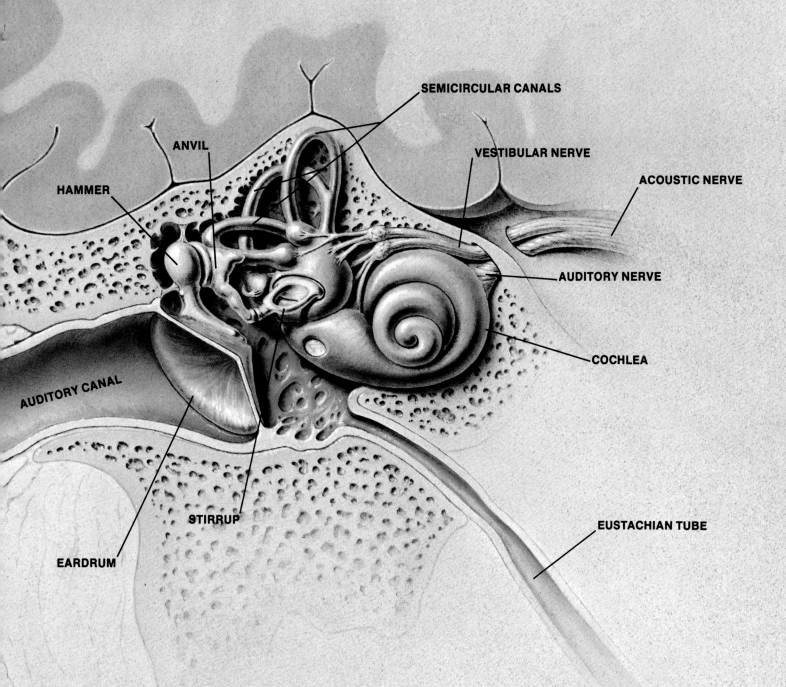

SEMICIRCULAR CANALS

ANVIL

VESTIBULAR NERVE

ACOUSTIC NERVE

HAMMER

AUDITORY NERVE

COCHLEA

AUDITORY CANAL

STIRRUP

EUSTACHIAN TUBE

EARDRUM

JANE HURD

Sounds of the world reach the brain through the ear. The auricle gathers sound waves and funnels them into the auditory canal. The sound waves strike the eardrum. This causes the eardrum to vibrate. Three tiny bones behind the eardrum—the hammer, the anvil, and the stirrup—pass the vibrations on to the cochlea. Inside the cochlea, hair cells change the vibrations into nerve impulses. The impulses travel to the brain through the auditory nerve. The eustachian tube links the ear and the throat. This tube opens automatically to keep the air pressure the same on both sides of the eardrum. Without equal pressure, the eardrum can't vibrate freely, and you can't hear so well as you normally do. Three semicircular canals help you keep your balance. They detect the movements of your head. Hair cells at one end of each canal send impulses through the vestibular nerve. The auditory and the vestibular nerves join to form the acoustic nerve.

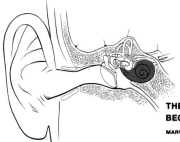

THE COCHLEA—WHERE VIBRATIONS BECOME NERVE IMPULSES

MARVIN J. FRYER

Vibrations in the air create nerve impulses inside the ear (below). Sound waves (indicated by purple arrows) strike the eardrum and set the three bones of the middle ear in motion. These tiny bones relay the vibrations of the eardrum to the inner ear through the oval window. The cochlea lies just on the other side of the oval window and is shaped like a spiral snail shell. In this drawing, it has been partly uncoiled. The cochlea contains three fluid-filled ducts, or tubes. One of these, the cochlear duct, has a flexible wall called the basilar (BAZ-uh-luhr) membrane. Tiny hair cells line this membrane. These cells make up the organ of Corti (KORT-ee). When sound vibrations pass through the oval window, they create waves in the fluid of the cochlea. The waves cause the basilar membrane to ripple. This movement bends the hair cells, setting off nerve impulses (shown by red arrows). Thousands of nerve fibers attached to the hair cells (only seven are shown here) pick up the impulses. The auditory nerve then carries the signals to the brain. When the waves reach the round window of the cochlea, they die away.

JANE HURD

For years, people enjoyed puzzling over this riddle: If a tree fell in a forest and no one was there to hear it crash, would there be any sound? We now know that the falling tree would cause sound waves. But if no ear was there to pick up those waves, they would be nothing more than vibrations in the air.

Sound waves result from the movement of an object, whether it is a tree falling or a door slamming. This movement causes the air—or other substances, such as water—to vibrate. Only when the ear picks up these vibrations and sends them as nerve impulses to the brain, do you hear them as sounds.

Scientists measure sound waves in two ways. One is to measure how many times the waves move back and forth each second. Most people can hear sound waves that vibrate from about 20 to 20,000 times a second. Waves that vibrate slowly produce low sounds, such as a deep hum. Rapidly vibrating waves produce high sounds, such as a shrill whistle.

Scientists also measure sound waves according to loudness. The scientists use a unit called the decibel (DESS-uh-bel) to describe how loud sounds are. The level of normal conversation is about 60 decibels. Experiments have shown that constant exposure to sounds above 80 decibels can cause loss of hearing. The louder the sound is,

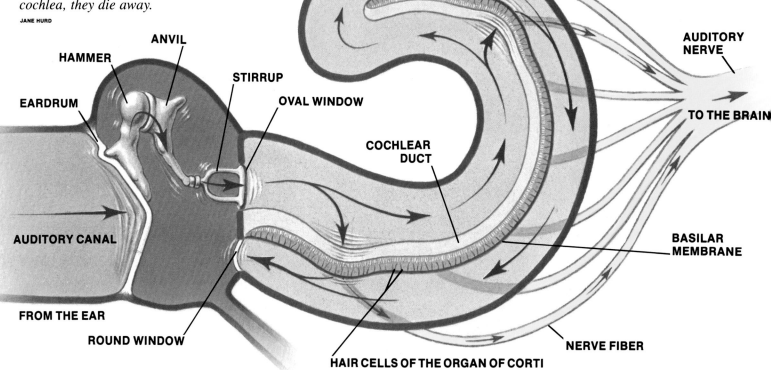

COCHLEA

AUDITORY NERVE

TO THE BRAIN

ANVIL

HAMMER

STIRRUP

EARDRUM

OVAL WINDOW

COCHLEAR DUCT

BASILAR MEMBRANE

AUDITORY CANAL

NERVE FIBER

FROM THE EAR

ROUND WINDOW

HAIR CELLS OF THE ORGAN OF CORTI

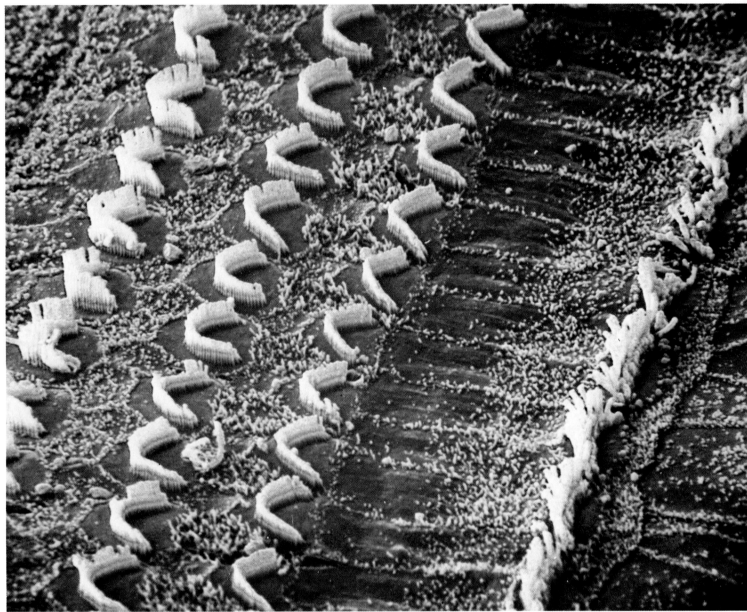

FROM *TISSUES AND ORGANS: A TEXT-ATLAS OF SCANNING ELECTRON MICROSCOPY* BY RICHARD G. KESSEL AND RANDY H. KARDON. W. H. FREEMAN AND COMPANY. COPYRIGHT © 1979

the less time it takes for damage to occur. Music at some rock concerts, for example, has been measured at as much as 120 decibels. Someone standing within inches of the speakers could experience permanent hearing loss almost immediately.

Vibrations of the air are not the only sounds you hear. You also pick up sounds through your skull. When you click your teeth or tap the top of your head, the sound waves vibrate through the bones of your skull. This explains why your voice may sound strange when you hear it on a tape recorder. When you talk, you hear your voice both through the air and through your skull. When you listen to a tape recording of your voice, you hear only the sound that is carried through the air. Sometimes people are surprised to find that, in a recording, their voices sound higher and much weaker than they would have thought.

Hair cells inside the ear resemble tracks left in the sand by truck tires. The cochlea contains about 15,000 hearing receptor cells arranged in four rows. In three of the rows, the hairs form V-shaped patterns. In the fourth row, shown here at right, the hairs stand in a straight line. The hair cells stick out from the basilar membrane. Sound waves cause this membrane to move up and down. The movement bends the hairs, which create nerve impulses. About 30,000 neurons and nerve fibers pick up the impulses and send them to the brain. Very loud sounds can actually destroy some of the hairs. Since they never grow back, permanent hearing loss results. The hair cells in this picture have been enlarged 4,000 times.

Students at Phillips Academy, in Andover, Massachusetts, take a canoe ride on a quiet autumn day. Their ears pick up a broad range of sounds.

Rustling leaves are among the faintest of the sounds the human ear can hear. You can tell where most sounds come from because you have two ears instead of

Mara Scheele, 11, of Arlington, Virginia, covers her ears as a jet roars overhead (above). The sound of something as noisy as a nearby jet can damage your ears. You can protect your hearing by avoiding extremely loud noises.

Sound Chart

Scientists measure the loudness of sounds in decibels. Here are the decibel levels of some common sounds:

Soft whisper 30	Loud alarm clock 80
Quiet room 40	Power mower 90
Running refrigerator 50	Chain saw 100
Normal conversation 60	Rock concert 120
Busy traffic 70	Jet plane 140

Warning: **The longer you listen to sounds louder than 80 decibels, the greater your chances are of damaging your hearing.**

one. When a sound comes from your left, for example, it reaches your left ear first. Your brain senses this and tells you that the sound came from your left.

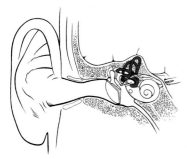

DELICATE ORGANS INSIDE THE INNER EAR HELP YOU MAINTAIN YOUR BALANCE.

Ballet students practice dance positions at the Washington School of the Ballet, in Washington, D.C. Ballet requires an excellent sense of balance. Dancers have to know the exact position of every part of their bodies. Organs of balance inside the ears of these young dancers keep track of every movement. When the brain receives signals from these organs, it orders the necessary muscles into action.

The Organs of Balance

Sit down. Stand up. Walk around. You do all three many times each day. A delicate system in your inner ear helps you do these ordinary things. It's called the vestibular (veh-STIB-yuh-ler) system. The vestibular system contains three structures that help you to keep your balance. The structures do this by detecting the movements and position of your head. One of the structures consists of three fluid-filled loops called the semicircular canals. Whenever you walk, bend over, or simply turn your head, the canals sense the movement.

Two other structures inside the ear record changes in the position of your head. These are the utricle and the saccule. Like the semicircular canals, these structures are filled with fluid. But they also contain tiny crystals embedded in a jelly-like membrane. The crystals respond to the pull of gravity or to any movement of the head.

The different balance organs provide different kinds of information. The semicircular canals send information to your brain when you turn your head in any direction. The utricle and saccule detect movements in a straight line and keep track of the position of your head.

If the organs of balance are ever damaged or destroyed by disease, the person affected may have some uncomfortable feelings. You've probably experienced temporary disturbances in your own sense of balance. For example, you may have become dizzy after whirling around and around. This happens because your whirling causes the fluid inside your semicircular canals to move. The fluid stays in motion for a few seconds even after you have stopped spinning. Your brain interprets this to mean that you're still moving. But your other senses tell your brain that you're now standing still. As a result, your brain is confused, and you feel dizzy.

Your brain relies on messages from other organs besides your ears to help you keep your balance. Your eyes and sense receptors in your muscles and joints send a constant stream of information to the brain about the position of your body. The brain studies these messages along with the signals from the ear's vestibular organs. It then issues commands that regulate the muscle movements necessary for you to keep your balance as you move around.

SISSE BRIMBERG/WOODFIN CAMP, INC.

A pretzel-shaped organ inside each ear helps you keep your body steady. The three fluid-filled loops of the semicircular canals contain hair receptor cells, somewhat like the cells you saw on page 77. Movement of the head causes the fluid in the loops to bend the hairs on these cells. The cells then send impulses that tell the brain which direction the head is turning. One canal is most sensitive to up-and-down movement (nodding "yes"). Another responds mostly to side-to-side motion (shaking "no"). The third canal reacts mainly when the head is tilted sideways.

© LENNART NILSSON/*BEHOLD MAN*/LITTLE, BROWN AND COMPANY, BOSTON

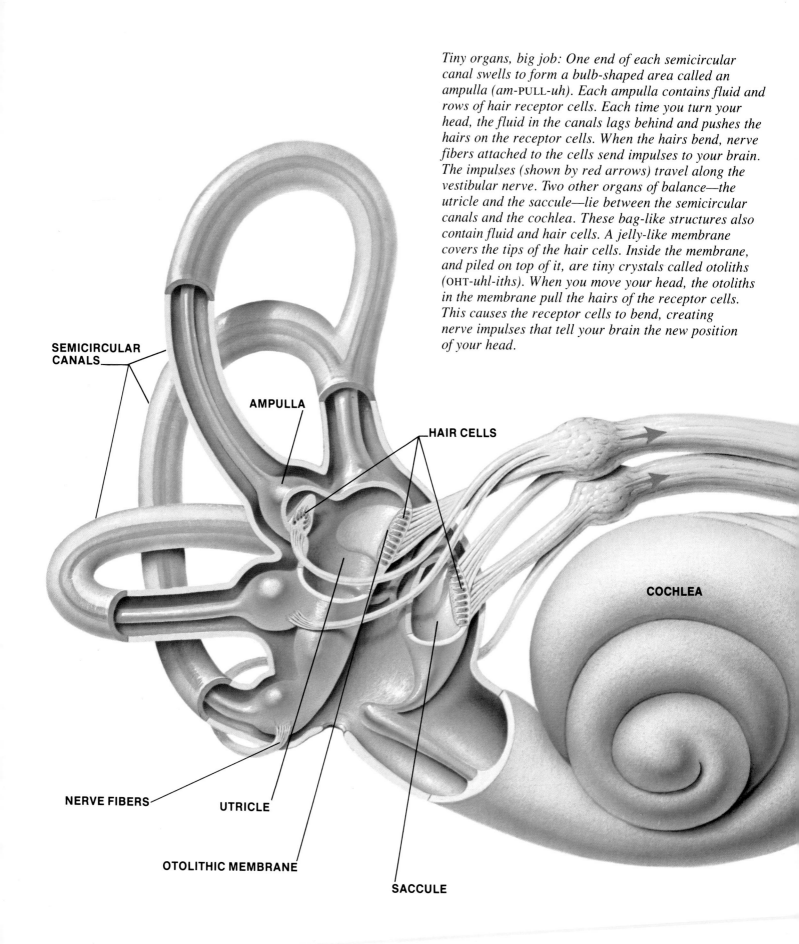

Tiny organs, big job: One end of each semicircular canal swells to form a bulb-shaped area called an ampulla (am-PULL-uh). Each ampulla contains fluid and rows of hair receptor cells. Each time you turn your head, the fluid in the canals lags behind and pushes the hairs on the receptor cells. When the hairs bend, nerve fibers attached to the cells send impulses to your brain. The impulses (shown by red arrows) travel along the vestibular nerve. Two other organs of balance—the utricle and the saccule—lie between the semicircular canals and the cochlea. These bag-like structures also contain fluid and hair cells. A jelly-like membrane covers the tips of the hair cells. Inside the membrane, and piled on top of it, are tiny crystals called otoliths (OHT-uhl-iths). When you move your head, the otoliths in the membrane pull the hairs of the receptor cells. This causes the receptor cells to bend, creating nerve impulses that tell your brain the new position of your head.

SEMICIRCULAR CANALS

AMPULLA

HAIR CELLS

COCHLEA

NERVE FIBERS

UTRICLE

OTOLITHIC MEMBRANE

SACCULE

Hair cells in the utricle and in the
saccule keep track of the position of your
head in relation to the ground. When the
girl at right stands upright, hair bundles
on the cells point straight into the
otolithic membrane (below).

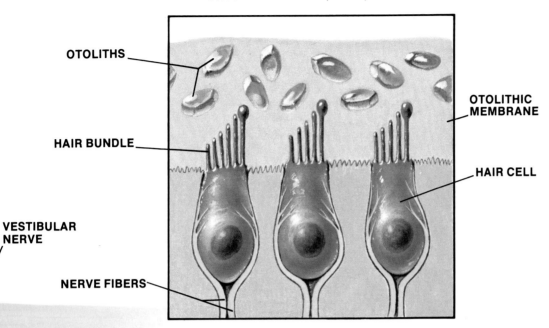

OTOLITHS

OTOLITHIC MEMBRANE

HAIR BUNDLE

HAIR CELL

VESTIBULAR NERVE

NERVE FIBERS

As the girl leans forward, the membrane
and otoliths move, too, but more slowly
than her head. This causes them to hold
back the hair bundles temporarily. Nerve
fibers on the hair cells sense this and
send out nerve impulses that tell the brain
the new position of the head.

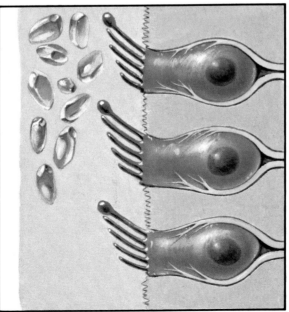

JANE HURD (ALL)

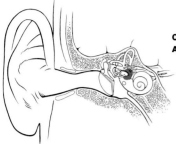

ORGANS OF BALANCE: THE UTRICLE AND SACCULE

You've probably seen pictures of astronauts floating in an orbiting space capsule. The astronauts float because there is no gravity in space to give their bodies weight. For a similar reason, there is no such thing as "up" or "down" in space. On earth, however, up and down have a lot of meaning. The parts of the ear that detect up and down—the utricle and saccule—provide your brain with such information by responding to the force of gravity.

Gravity pulls against the otoliths, or small crystals, inside the utricle and saccule. The shifting otoliths create nerve impulses that travel to the brain along the vestibular nerve. They tell the brain about the position of your head in relation to the ground. Because of these impulses, your brain can help you do such things as walk across a dark room without toppling over.

Otoliths like these rest on top of hair cells in the utricle and the saccule. These tiny crystals respond to the pull of gravity and to any movement of the head. Otoliths are too small to see with the unaided eye. A microscope was used to produce this image.

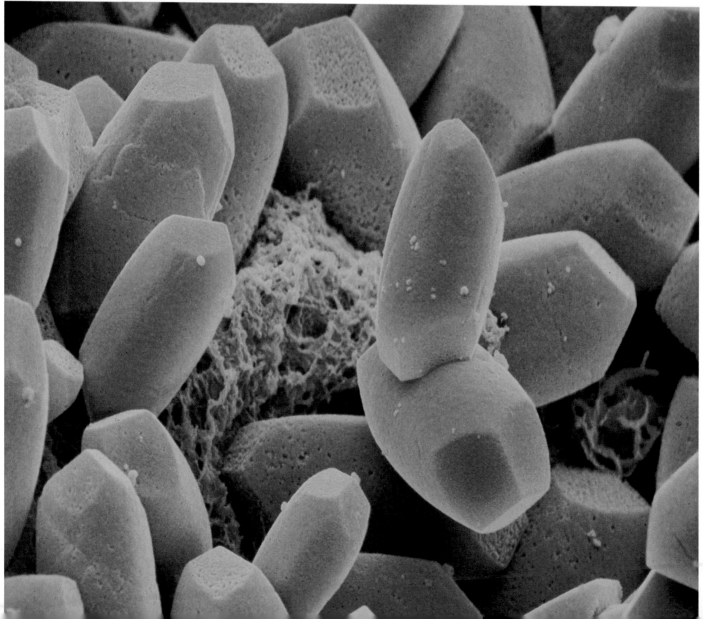

FROM *TISSUES AND ORGANS: A TEXT-ATLAS OF SCANNING ELECTRON MICROSCOPY* BY RICHARD G. KESSEL AND RANDY H. KARDON. W.H. FREEMAN AND COMPANY. COPYRIGHT © 1979

Like rows of cactuses, hair cells in the ear (above) stand up to receive signals from otoliths. In this photograph, the layer of otoliths has been removed. Each cell contains hairs of different lengths, with one hair longer than the rest. This long hair helps regulate the nerve impulses sent out by the cell. When otoliths bend a cell's hairs in the direction of the longest hair, the cell sends out more impulses. When otoliths bend the hairs away from the longest hair, the cell sends out fewer impulses. This tells the brain that the head is moving in a particular direction. These hair cells have been magnified 5,300 times.

Circus performers thrill a crowd in Landover, Maryland, with their balancing act (below). Originally from Poland, the men and women of the Oblocki Troupe are members of the Ringling Brothers and Barnum & Bailey Circus. Performers such as these develop their sense of balance through years of practice. Some experienced tightrope walkers can even do a backflip while walking on a high wire.

N.G.S. PHOTOGRAPHER JOSEPH H. BAILEY

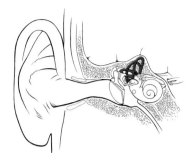

ORGANS OF BALANCE: SEMICIRCULAR CANALS

Always busy, tiny hair cells inside the semicircular canals keep your brain informed about where you're headed. The hair cells are found in the ampulla, a rounded area at one end of each canal. Fluid inside the canals causes the hairs on the cells to move back and forth when you move, creating nerve impulses that race to the brain.

The three loops of the semicircular canals sit at right angles, like a floor and two walls in the corner of a room. Because of this, the loops can pick up movement in any direction. The canals work in pairs. A loop in one ear teams with a loop in the opposite ear.

For example, when you tilt your head, a canal in each ear detects the motion. Both canals signal the brain. Say you tilt your head to the right. Your right ear sends many nerve impulses. Your left ear sends fewer impulses. The brain compares the number of signals from each ear to tell you which way you're moving.

The semicircular canals, together with the utricle and saccule, give your brain information about the position and movement of your head.

Tangled hair cells (above) sense the direction and speed of your movements. Hair cells like the ones in this photograph are found in the bulb-shaped ampulla at one end of each semicircular canal. Turning your head causes the fluid inside the canals to move about. This bends the hairs of the cells back and forth, like seaweed waving in an ocean current. The hair cells tell the brain which way you're moving—and at what speed.

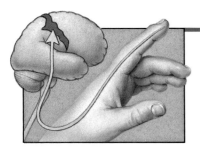

Touch: Messages of Feeling

SENSE RECEPTORS IN OR BENEATH THE SKIN DETECT TOUCH—OR PRESSURE—TEMPERATURE, AND INJURY. MESSAGES FROM THESE RECEPTORS TRAVEL TO THE SOMATOSENSORY (SOH-MAT-UH-SENSE-UH-REE) CORTEX. THE BRAIN THEN TRANSLATES THEM INTO SUCH SENSATIONS AS TOUCH-PRESSURE, WARMTH, COOLNESS, AND PAIN.

People like to be touched. That's one reason why, when people meet, they greet each other by shaking hands. It's why you feel good when someone gives you a pat on the back after you've done a good job. Or why you show friends you like them by giving them a hug.

People also NEED to be touched. Doctors say that babies are healthier if their parents pick them up and hold them regularly. For a newborn baby, touch is perhaps the most important sense. From the moment it is born, a baby begins using the sense of touch to find out about the world.

Throughout your life, touch brings you an endless flow of information about the things around you. For example, sense receptors in or beneath your skin send information to the brain, which then tells you whether something is hard or soft, hot or cold, pleasant or painful.

Other receptors inform you of what is happening inside your body. Those in your muscles and joints tell your brain about the position and movement of your arms and legs. Certain receptors in internal organs detect changes in pressure. They send out messages of pain—a headache or a stomach-ache, for example—when problems exist.

There are many thousands of tiny sense receptors scattered all over your body. A nerve fiber links each receptor to your spinal cord or brain stem. From there, other nerve cells transmit the messages up to your brain. Every time you touch something, the receptors send messages that tell the brain you are feeling something. Then the brain figures out what the sensation actually is.

Scientists have discovered several different kinds of receptors in the skin. Some detect touch-pressure. Others respond to changes in temperature. The purpose of certain receptors is still unknown. Although much about the sense of touch remains a mystery, its importance in helping us feel the world around us is no secret.

Resembling an onion, a touch-pressure receptor known as a Pacinian (puh-CHEE-nee-uhn) corpuscle detects rapid changes in pressure, such as vibration. Layers of tissue and fluid surrounding a single nerve fiber make up the corpuscle, shown here in cross section. When something strikes or pushes against the flexible walls of the corpuscle, the nerve fiber fires electrical signals. Other kinds of receptors respond to temperature or to injury. Receptors for touch-pressure, temperature, and injury exist throughout your body. Many are in or beneath your skin. These tiny receptors inform the brain of everything your body touches.

J. F. GENNARO; L. R. GRILLONE/PHOTO RESEARCHERS, INC.

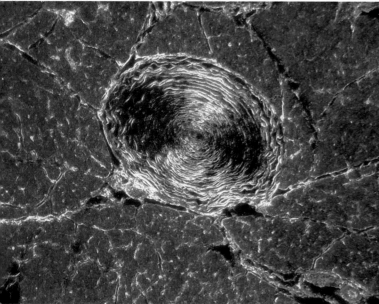

A successful catch for Billy Britt, 10, of Ocala, Florida, (right) began with the sense of touch. Receptors in Billy's hands enabled him to feel his fishing rod vibrate when the fish bit the hook. Because this fish is small, Billy's grandfather, Homer Circle, will release it. Receptors that detect touch-pressure and temperature allow us to feel the world around us. For example, temperature receptors tell Billy and his grandfather that the water is cool and that the sun feels warm.

JAMES H. KARALES/PETER ARNOLD, INC.

Signals From Your Skin

The organs of vision, smell, taste, hearing, and balance are located only in the head. But touch-pressure, temperature, and injury receptors cover every inch of your body.

Any part of your skin can detect touch-pressure, temperature, or injury. However, the different kinds of receptors are not spread evenly over your body. For example, the skin of your fingertips contains many more sense receptors than an equal area on your arm contains. These make your fingertips more sensitive to touch than your arm is. Other areas contain even fewer sense receptors.

Doctors can measure how sensitive different areas of skin are. They do this with an instrument that looks somewhat like a drawing compass. The instrument has two points that can be set different distances apart.

To test sense receptors in a specific area, the doctors touch the area with the instrument. At first, they set the points together. The doctors gradually open the points until the person being tested feels two touch sensations instead of one. The skin of the fingertips can detect the two points when they are about as close together as 2/25 of an inch (2 mm). That distance is about equal to the thickness of 23 sheets in this book. In some areas of the back, the points can be nearly 3 inches (8 cm) apart before a person can feel them as two distinct sensations.

Because receptors are found all over the body, many have to send their messages long distances. The pathway from your eyes to your brain may be only a few inches long. But the nerve pathway between your brain and the receptors in your toes may be several feet long.

Think what happens when your toes make a "long-distance call" to your brain. Say an insect lands on your left big toe. Here's what takes place in a fraction of a second: Receptors in your toe create nerve impulses. The impulses travel along nerve fibers in the foot and leg. Finally the impulses reach the nerve cells of the spinal cord or the brain stem. Other cells then forward the information to other regions of the brain. Because most sensory nerve signals cross in the spinal cord or brain stem, the message from your left big toe finally reaches the right half of your brain. The message travels to an area within your brain called the somatosensory cortex.

When the touch-pressure signal arrives, your brain studies it. Then it issues a command that tells your body what to do—in this case, to brush the insect off your toe. You automatically know which toe to brush. That's because receptors in each part of your body send their signals to a specific area of the somatosensory cortex. The drawing on page 91 shows where touch messages from the various parts of your body arrive in your brain.

Touch-pressure messages travel first to the brain stem and then to the thalamus, a higher relay station. The thalamus in turn sends the information to a narrow strip of the brain called the somatosensory cortex (right). This drawing shows the somatosensory cortex in the left half of the brain. Signals from the right side of the body travel there. Receptors in each part of the body send signals to a specific section of the cortex. The upper part of the drawing shows how much of the cortex is devoted to the various parts of the body. Sensitive areas such as your hands contain many sense receptors in a small area. A large portion of the somatosensory cortex receives messages from the hands. Other sensitive areas include the face and the feet. These also require a large area of the cortex to receive their messages. Areas of the skin less crowded with receptors need smaller areas of the cortex to receive their signals. The oddly shaped figure below shows how a person would look if the parts of the body were in proportion to the amount of the somatosensory cortex devoted to them. It shows that—to your somatosensory cortex—your hands, face, and feet are the most important parts of your body.

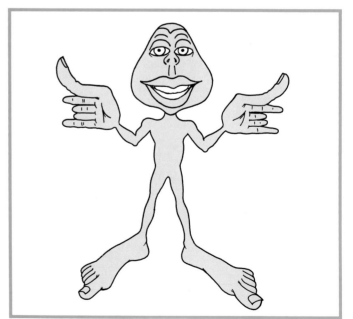

MARVIN J. FRYER (ABOVE AND OPPOSITE)

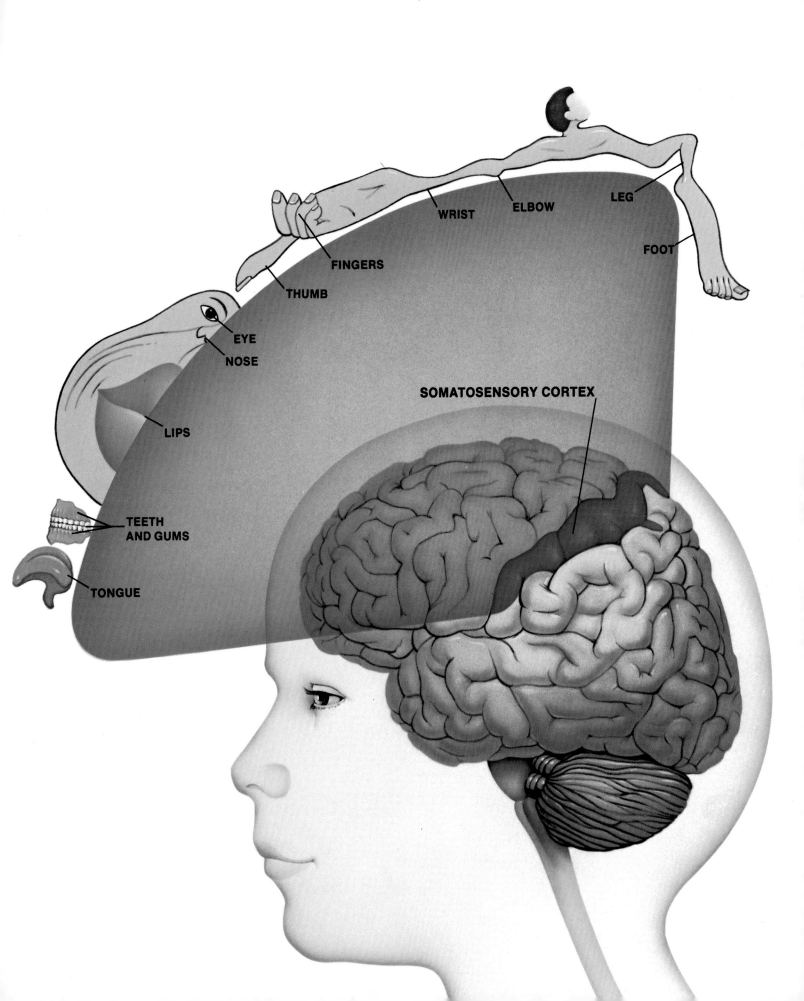

WRIST
ELBOW
LEG
FOOT
FINGERS
THUMB
EYE
NOSE
SOMATOSENSORY CORTEX
LIPS
TEETH
AND GUMS
TONGUE

Sensitive fingertips feel warmth and smoothness as Sandra Cummer, 13, pets her family's pony, Thunder (left). Sandra can feel the temperature and texture of Thunder's nose because of sense receptors in her skin. The pony seems to enjoy Sandra's attention. "He's our friend and he likes to be petted," she says. Sandra lives near Sherrill, Iowa.

The Many Messages of Touch

The thousands of receptors lying in or beneath your skin all send information to your brain in the form of electrical and chemical impulses. Sensory nerves are actually the axons of nerve cells whose cell bodies are located just outside the spinal cord or brain stem. Touch receptors form the endings of some of these nerves. The nerve endings react each time something comes into contact with your skin.

Capsule-like structures called end organs surround some nerve endings. Scientists believe the end organs transmit information to the nerve endings. For example, the sense receptor called a Pacinian corpuscle responds to vibration. Layers of tissue and fluid form a capsule around the nerve ending in this receptor. Pressure from objects you touch pushes the flexible walls of the capsule out of shape. The nerve ending inside the capsule detects this and creates electrical impulses. Structures that surround other kinds of nerve endings transmit information in other ways.

End organs do not surround all nerve endings, however. Sensory nerves without specialized end organs are known as free nerve endings. Free nerve endings are tiny branching fibers. Scientists believe that different types of free nerve endings are responsible for detecting injury, warmth, and coolness.

Sense receptors often get used to the feel of an object

A section of a fingertip shows the skin's structure (right). The protective outer layer is called the epidermis (ep-uh-DER-mus). The dermis (DER-mus) contains sweat glands that help cool the skin, as well as blood vessels that bring it food. The subcutaneous (sub-kew-TAY-nee-uhs) tissue, a layer of fat, helps insulate the skin. All three layers contain sense receptors called nerve endings. These are connected to nerve cells with cell bodies outside the spinal cord or brain stem. Many of the sense receptors are named for scientists who discovered them. Pacinian corpuscles, Meissner's corpuscles, Ruffini's endings, and Merkel's disks detect touch-pressure. Different kinds of free nerve endings are believed to detect cooling, warming, or injury. Scientists are not sure what the receptors called Krause's end bulbs are sensitive to. Impulses from all these receptors travel to the spinal cord or the brain stem along sensory nerves like the one shown here.
JANE HURD

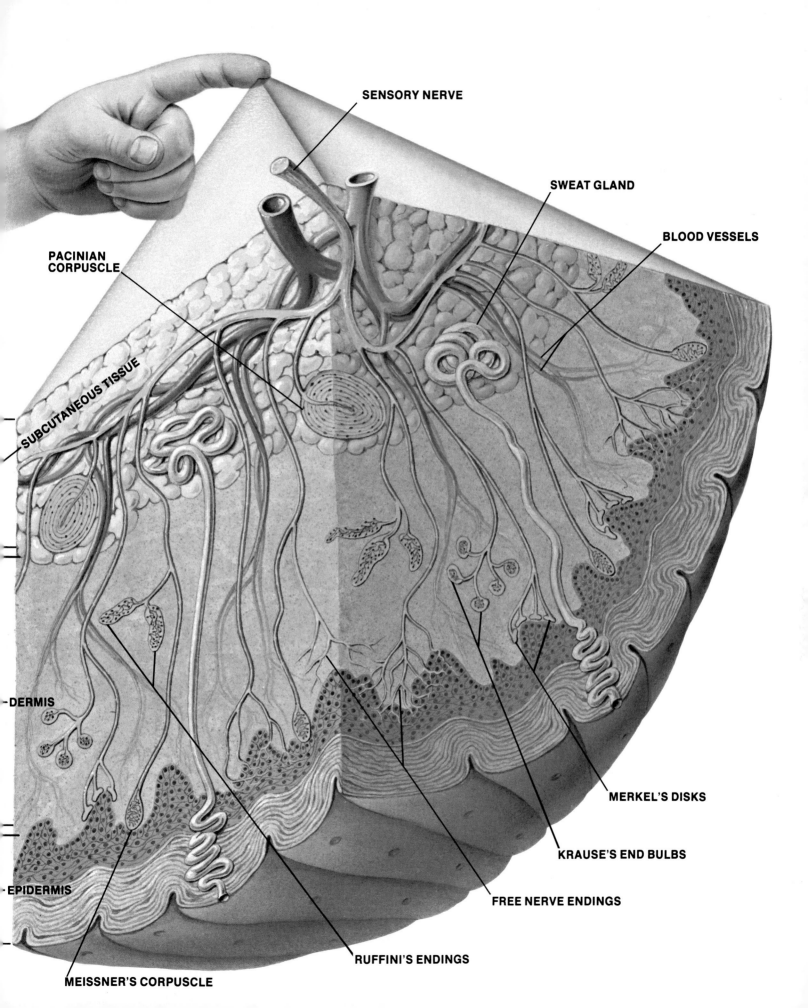

SENSORY NERVE

SWEAT GLAND

BLOOD VESSELS

PACINIAN
CORPUSCLE

SUBCUTANEOUS TISSUE

DERMIS

EPIDERMIS

MERKEL'S DISKS

KRAUSE'S END BULBS

FREE NERVE ENDINGS

RUFFINI'S ENDINGS

MEISSNER'S CORPUSCLE

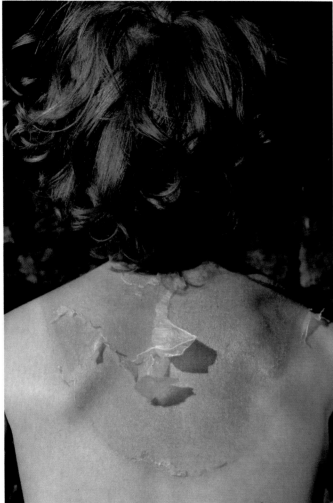

over a period of time. This is called adapting. Some touch-pressure receptors adapt quickly. Others adapt slowly. For example, if you hold a pet turtle in your hand, you can feel its pressure against your skin. When you first pick up the turtle, all the touch-pressure receptors in or beneath the skin of your hand will respond. However, some of the receptors will stop responding as long as the turtle stays still. These touch-pressure receptors—Pacinian corpuscles, for example—adapt quickly to steady pressure. But if the turtle should suddenly move, they will quickly respond. Other touch-pressure receptors, such as Merkel's disks, adapt slowly to steady pressure. These receptors continue to send impulses that inform your brain that there's something pressing on your hand, even if the turtle doesn't move.

One sensation you usually do not get used to is pain. Injury signals are important because they tell your brain something harmful or possibly damaging is happening to your body—and that you should do something right away to protect yourself.

Scientists classify pain in two broad categories: superficial—surface—pain and deep pain. Superficial pain is what you feel when you stick your finger with a needle. It often consists of a brief pricking sensation followed by a longer-lasting burning sensation. Deep pain is the aching, general pain you feel when you sprain your ankle.

Sometimes you may feel pain even when there is no injury. For example, sometimes a blood vessel in your head may expand a little more than usual. This activates receptors that respond to expansion or pressure. As a result, you feel a headache.

D.H.THOMPSON/OXFORD SCIENTIFIC FILMS

Severe sunburn means pain for a young girl (above). Her red, peeling skin has been damaged by too much exposure to the ultraviolet rays of the sun. Pain from this sort of injury lasts a long time. Injury receptors in the girl's skin will continue sending out impulses until the skin begins to heal. The skin has no receptors to warn of overexposure to the sun before the damage has been done.

Receptors in the skin flash a message of pain when the body is injured. Scientists believe these receptors, called free nerve endings, respond when something that might harm the body touches the skin. Messages from the receptors (red arrows) travel to the brain along nerve fibers. A fatty material called myelin (MY-uh-luhn) surrounds the bottom fiber. This material increases the speed of nerve impulses.

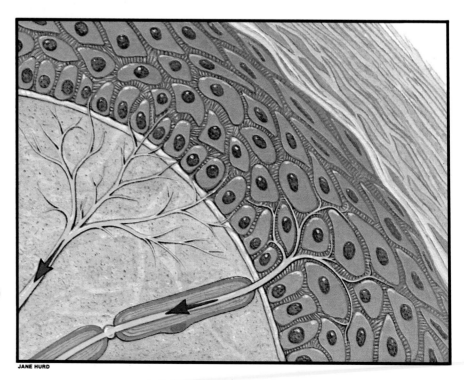

JANE HURD

Ouch! Sallie Cummer reacts with an expression of pain as she catches her skin on a fence. "I was crawling through the fence because I didn't want to open the gate," said Sallie. "I got caught in the barbed wire, and it hurt." Sometimes a sharp poke on the skin causes two kinds of pain. First you feel a brief pricking pain. Then you feel a longer lasting, burning pain. That is because the first kind of pain travels along myelinated nerve fibers and reaches the brain quickly. The second kind travels along non-myelinated fibers and moves more slowly.

Your Senses at Work

For some people, the sense of touch does more than tell them if objects are hard or soft. Many blind people rely on the sense of touch to learn more about the world in which they live. These people use their sense of touch to read.

Some blind people read thanks to a special printing system called Braille. A page printed in Braille has small raised dots in place of letters printed on paper. People read the page by touching the raised dots with their fingertips.

Blind people learn to concentrate on their sense of touch because they rely heavily on it. This is an example of how we learn to adapt if one sense is unable to function properly. People learn to rely more on their other senses when one sense is denied them.

Many people can develop their senses if they practice using them. For example, professional tea tasters develop an excellent sense of smell and taste. From the aroma and taste of a sample of tea, they can name the country from which the tea leaves came. People who create perfumes develop an extra-fine sense of smell. With a single sniff, perfumers can pick out one ingredient from a mixture containing hundreds of ingredients.

Musicians become expert at singling out the sounds of individual instruments in an orchestra. An artist can see the difference between shades of paint that might look the same to most observers. Through years of practice, people develop the senses they need most.

You may find that one or more of your senses will begin to change as you grow older. You may become like a grandparent whose sight or hearing is not so good as it once was. This is part of life—something that most of us will experience. Devices such as eyeglasses and hearing aids can often help people overcome problems with their senses.

Vision, taste, smell, hearing, and touch all work hard for you. From the moment you were born, you began experiencing the world through your senses. And every day of your life, you will continue to rely on them.

Flames leap from a cabin during a presentation of "The Shepherd of the Hills," a play set in the Ozark region of Missouri (left). An actor tries to put out the fire with a bucket of water. This fire was set on purpose as part of the play. Although it's just a make-believe scene, the intense heat from the fire is real. In the actor's skin, free nerve endings that respond to painful heat warn his body about the hot temperatures.

N.G.S.PHOTOGRAPHER BRUCE DALE (OPPOSITE)

A snow-covered window feels cold to the touch of Joe Habel, 14, of Holy Cross, Iowa (right). Free nerve endings in Joe's fingertips detect cold temperatures. Joe uses more than his sense of touch while he stands at the window. As he listens for the sounds of his school bus, he watches his pet geese and ducks play in the snow. Touch, hearing, and vision —all part of his fantastic five senses— provide Joe's real window on the world.

Your Senses...and Beyond

As you read this book, you learned many things about your sense receptors and your nervous system. You found out that receptors detect what is happening around you. You discovered that nerve impulses are transmitted from your sense receptors to your brain. And you learned that the brain helps control your entire body by interpreting these messages and sending out commands.

Although you've learned a lot, there is still much more to discover about your fantastic five senses. Many scientists spend their lives studying just one of the body's sense receptors. Researchers are continually trying to find out new things about the brain and the senses. In space, as the space shuttle *Columbia* circled the earth in December l983, scientists conducted experiments involving the balance receptors of the inner ear. They sought to discover what causes spacesickness, a feeling of nausea and dizziness that often affects astronauts.

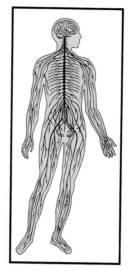

THE BODY'S COMPLEX COMMUNICATIONS NETWORK—THE BRAIN, SPINAL CORD, PERIPHERAL NERVES, AND SENSE RECEPTORS— ENABLES YOU TO EXPERIENCE THE WORLD AND REACT TO IT.

A Matter of Taste

Many scientists today are concerned about how we will feed the world's growing population. There are more than 4½ billion humans on earth today, and that number grows by about 82 million each year. As the earth's population increases, new sources of food must be found.

Taste researchers are working on solutions to this problem. By studying the flavors people like and finding ways to create them, scientists hope to make the taste of new food sources more acceptable to humans.

Sniffing Out Facts

Researchers today are discovering more about how odors help control human behavior. Studies have shown that people may be able to identify other people by smell alone. It could be that people are somehow attracted to one another by odors they are unaware of.

Human odors are important for other reasons. Certain diseases—diabetes, for example—can be detected by analyzing the smell of a person's breath. Researchers are now studying new ways of using body odors to help doctors recognize and treat a variety of illnesses.

Treating Eye Diseases

Doctors have already found an effective tool—the laser— for treating many kinds of eye diseases. With the specially focused high intensity light beam created by the laser, doctors can now weld rips in the retina, seal leaking blood vessels, and vaporize cancerous tissue. They can open pathways to drain off excess fluid inside the eyeball. Before the

laser came into use, treating these eye conditions was much more difficult. Scientists are working to discover other uses the laser might have in treating diseases—not just in the eye, but in other parts of the body as well.

Touching the Future

Many things remain to be discovered about the sense of touch. For example, scientists want to know more about how messages of injury are transmitted to the brain and analyzed. One of their goals is to discover new ways of controlling sensations of pain. Researchers have shown that the brain itself naturally contains substances that may act to reduce pain sensations.

Studying the Brain

For many researchers, the brain is the most challenging part of the body's communications network. Scientists

have discovered much concerning the structure of the brain. But many mysteries remain about how the brain works. For example, no one yet knows how the brain recognizes objects, or just how memory occurs. Scientists are still trying to find out how the brain controls reasoning, imagination, and emotions.

Why are some people more intelligent or more creative than others? What shapes a person's personality? How are humans aware of themselves as individuals? Questions like these have interested people for centuries. Yet the answers to such questions are still being sought.

Finally, About Your Other Senses

After all you have read, would you be surprised now to learn that you actually have more than five senses? You have already read about one of them—the vestibular system that sends messages to your brain concerning the position and movement of your head. Scientists believe that humans have many other senses—perhaps twenty or more. Many of these senses work without your being aware of them. Vision, taste, smell, hearing, and touch are only the senses people know best.

Special sense receptors detect things that happen inside your body. For example, some of these receptors detect the pressure of the blood that flows through your body. They also measure how much sugar the blood contains. Others, located in your muscles and joints, detect the position and movement of parts of your body, such as your arms and legs.

A simple experiment will make you aware of some of these receptors at work. Just close your eyes and try to touch the tip of your left index finger to that of your right index finger. More than likely, you will be able to do this in one or two tries. You're able to touch your fingertips together without looking because of sense receptors that detect the position and movement of your arms and fingers.

Messages from receptors such as these are just as important as messages from other senses. Your brain uses information from every sense organ to help regulate your body. Scientists may discover even more senses in the future. Perhaps some day you will read a book about your fantastic 50 senses!

A watery ride brings the senses alive for Helima Croft, at left, and Alexa Johnstone, both 12. Helima and Alexa enjoy the thrilling ride at an amusement park in Virginia.
PAT LANZA FIELD

Glossary

acoustic nerve — the nerve that is formed by the combination of the vestibular and auditory nerves; it carries messages of hearing and balance from the inner ear to the brain

ampulla — a bulb-shaped enlargement at one end of a semicircular canal that contains hair receptor cells

anvil — one of three small bones in the middle ear

association areas — areas of the cerebral cortex that analyze, process, and probably store information they receive from the sense receptors and from other areas of the cortex

auditory canal — the part of the outer ear through which sound waves travel to reach the eardrum

auditory cortex — the part of the cerebral cortex that is the primary receiving area for nerve impulses from the organ of Corti in the inner ear

auditory nerve — the nerve that carries signals from the organ of Corti in the inner ear toward the brain

auricle — the visible ear, the flap of skin on each side of your head

autonomic nervous system — the portion of the peripheral nervous system concerned with regulating "automatic" actions within the body, such as breathing, heart rate, and food digestion

axon — a fiber extending from a neuron that passes messages on to other neurons

basilar membrane — the flexible membrane in the cochlea that supports the organ of Corti in the inner ear

blind spot — the point where the optic nerve leaves the eye; here, there are no rods or cones to respond to light

brain stem — the part of the brain between the spinal cord and the cerebral hemispheres

central nervous system — the brain and spinal cord, which receive information from the sense receptors, process it, and send motor impulses to the muscles

cerebral cortex — the outer layer of the cerebral hemispheres that is responsible for such mental functions as thinking, remembering, and imagining, and also for movement and other behaviors

cerebrum — the main part of the brain, where thinking, learning, and remembering take place; it is divided in the middle, and its two halves make up about two-thirds of your brain

chemical sensors — sense receptors in your mouth and nose that respond to chemical substances in the food you eat or in the air you breathe

choroid — a thin, pigmented layer of tissue that coats the eye and supplies the outer retina with nourishment

cilia — tiny hair-like extensions on the surfaces of some cells

cochlea — the coil-shaped structure of the inner ear in which sound waves become nerve impulses

cochlear duct — one of three ducts, or tubes, that make up the cochlea

color blindness — the inability to distinguish between two or more colors because of defects in one type of cone in the retina or because of problems with processing the signals that give color vision

cornea — a transparent layer on the front of the eye that helps focus light rays entering the eye

corpus callosum — a large bundle of nerve fibers that connects the left and right cerebral hemispheres

decibel — a unit used to measure the loudness of sounds

dendrites — small, thin extensions of the neuron that receive impulses from other neurons and pass them on to the cell body

eardrum — a thin, flexible membrane that separates the outer ear from the middle ear

epiglottis — a flap of tissue-covered cartilage in the throat that covers the opening to the lungs and prevents food from entering the lungs when swallowing

eustachian tube — a tube linking the middle ear and the throat that equalizes the air pressure on both sides of the eardrum

farsightedness — a condition in which distant objects are seen clearly but nearby objects appear blurred, because light rays from nearby objects come to focus behind the retina instead of on it

fovea — a small depression in the retina in which there is a high concentration of cone cells; there, the retina produces its sharpest and clearest vision

free nerve endings — sense receptors that respond to warmth, coolness, or injury to the body

glia — special nerve cells that support and nourish neurons

gustatory cortex — the part of the cerebral cortex that is the main receiving area for messages from taste receptors in the mouth

hair cells — cells in the inner ear that pick up movement and pass it on to nerve fibers, to be carried to the brain in the form of nerve impulses

hammer — the outermost of three tiny bones in the middle ear

inner ear — the part of the ear that contains the organ of hearing, called the organ of Corti, and the organs of balance — the semicircular canals, the utricle, and the saccule

iris — the colored part of the eye around the pupil that changes in size to regulate the amount of light passing to the retina

lens — a curved, transparent structure behind the pupil and iris of the eye that focuses light rays onto the retina

Meissner's corpuscles — sense receptors in the skin that respond to touch-pressure

melanin — dark pigment that colors your hair, skin, and eyes; in the eyes, melanin helps protect sensitive tissues from bright light

Merkel's disks — sense receptors in the skin that respond to touch-pressure

middle ear — a small chamber between the eardrum and the cochlea that contains three small bones — the hammer, the anvil, and the stirrup

motor nerves — nerves that carry messages from the central nervous system to the muscles and organs of the body

mucus — a thick, slippery substance produced by special cells in the body; it protects and moistens fragile tissue

myelin — a fatty white material that covers the axons of some nerves; it helps speed nerve impulses along the pathways to and from the brain

nearsightedness — a condition in which nearby objects appear clear and distant objects look blurred, because light rays from distant objects come into focus in front of rather than on the retina

nervous system — the brain, spinal cord, and network of nerves that make up the body's internal communications network

neuron — the conducting cell of the nervous system, typically made up of a cell body, dendrites, and one or more axons

neurotransmitters — chemical messengers, stored in the vesicles at synapses, that transmit the electrical signal of one neuron to another neuron

olfactory bulb — an area of the brain that relays messages from the smell receptors in the nose to other areas of the brain

olfactory cortex — the main receiving area of the cerebral cortex for smell information from the nose

olfactory epithelium — patches of delicate tissue inside the upper part of each nasal passage that contain smell receptors and mucus-secreting Bowman's glands

optic chiasm — the area of the brain in which some nerve fibers from each eye cross in an X-shape; the fibers from the right side of each eye go to the right side of the brain, and fibers from the left sides go to the left side of the brain

optic nerve — the nerve that carries messages from the eye into the brain

organ of Corti — a part of the inner ear which contains hair cells that send nerve impulses through the auditory nerve to the brain

otolithic membrane — a jelly-like layer of tissue in the utricle and saccule that contains otoliths, tiny crystals

outer ear — the auricle and the auditory canal; the auricle gathers sound waves in the air and directs them through the auditory canal to the eardrum

Pacinian corpuscle — a touch-pressure receptor that responds to rapid changes in pressure, such as vibration

papillae — groups of taste buds in the mouth, especially on the surface of the tongue

peripheral nervous system — the network of nerves throughout the body that carries messages to and from the central nervous system

peripheral vision — the outer edge of the field of vision

pigments — substances in the tissues that give them color

pupil — the opening in the iris that regulates the amount of light entering the eye

retina — a light-sensitive layer of nerve tissue that lines the eye, in which images are translated into electrical signals and transmitted to the brain

rhodopsin — a light-sensitive pigment in the rod cells of the eye

rods and cones — special receptor cells in the retina that respond to light and change it into electrical impulses

Ruffini's endings — sense receptors in the skin that respond to touch-pressure

sclera — the tough white coat that covers most of the eyeball

semicircular canals — three fluid-filled loops in the inner ear that contain sense receptors; the receptors detect the movement and the position of the head

sense receptors — cells that respond to stimulation from such things as sounds or pressure or light

sensory nerves — nerves that carry messages from sense receptors to the central nervous system

somatosensory cortex — the primary receiving area of the cerebral cortex for messages from the sense receptors in or beneath the skin

stirrup — the innermost of three tiny bones in the middle ear

synapse — the point between neurons where electrical signals from one are passed on to the second by the release of a chemical transmitter

synaptic vesicle — the tiny chemical-filled sac in the tip of an axon where transmitters are stored

taste buds — tiny taste organs in the mouth that respond to chemical substances in food and drink

thalamus — a structure on the top of the brain stem that is the main relay center for sensory impulses and information from the body to the cerebral cortex

utricle and saccule — two bag-like structures in the inner ear that provide information about the position and the movement of the head

vestibular nerve — the nerve that carries signals from the vestibular system of the inner ear toward the brain

visual cortex — the primary receiving area of the cerebral cortex for visual information from the retina of the eye

vitreous body — the clear jelly that fills the eyeball

Index

Bold type refers to illustrations;
regular type refers to text.

CONSULTANTS

Janett Trubatch, Ph.D., National Institutes of Health, *Chief Consultant*

Glenn O. Blough, LL.D., University of Maryland, *Educational Consultant*

Lynda Ehrlich, Montgomery County (Maryland) Public Schools, *Reading Consultant*

Phyllis G. Sidorsky, National Cathedral School, *Consulting Librarian*

Nicholas J. Long, Ph.D., *Consulting Psychologist*

The Special Publications and School Services Division is grateful to the individuals and organizations listed here for their generous cooperation and assistance during the preparation of *MESSENGERS TO THE BRAIN:*

David R. Christman, Brookhaven National Laboratory; Israel Goldberg, National Institutes of Health; Peter B. Johnsen, Monell Chemical Senses Center; Robert H. LaMotte, Yale University School of Medicine; Ralph F. Naunton, National Institutes of Health; David A. Newsome, Johns Hopkins Medical Institutions; Wesley Norman, Georgetown University; Michael E. Phelps, UCLA School of Medicine.

ADDITIONAL READING

Readers may want to check the National Geographic Index in a school or a public library for related articles and to refer to the following books. ("A" indicates a book for readers at the adult level.)

Adler, Irving and Ruth, *Taste, Touch and Smell,* Harper & Row Publishers, Inc., 1966. Aliki, *My Five Senses,* Harper & Row Publishers, Inc., 1972. Allison, Linda, *Blood and Guts: A Working Guide to Your Own Little Insides,* Little, Brown, and Co., 1976. Bruun, Ruth D. and Bertel, *The Human Body,* Random House, Inc., 1982. Cobb, Vicki, *How to Really Fool Yourself: Illusions for All Your Senses,* Harper & Row Publishers, Inc., 1981. Facklam, Margery and Howard, *The Brain: Magnificent Mind Machine,* Harcourt Brace Jovanovich, Inc., 1982. *Frontiers of Science,* National Geographic Society, 1982 (A). Hyman, June, *Deafness,* Franklin Watts, Inc., 1980. Miller, Jonathan, *The Human Body* (a pop-up book), Viking Press, Inc., 1983 (A). Murphy, Wendy B., *Touch, Smell, Taste, Sight and Hearing,* Time-Life Books, 1982 (A). Nourse, Alan E., *The Body,* Time-Life Books, 1980. Rahn, Joan E., *Eyes and Seeing,* Atheneum Publishers, 1981. Stevens, S. S. and Fred Warshofsky, *Sound and Hearing,* Time-Life Books, 1980 (A). Ward, Brian, *The Eye and Sight,* Franklin Watts, Inc., 1981. Ward, Brian, *The Ear and Hearing,* Franklin Watts, Inc., 1981. *Your Wonderful Body,* National Geographic Society, 1982. Zim, Herbert S., *Your Brain and How It Works,* William Morrow & Co., Inc., 1972.

Library of Congress CIP Data
Main entry under title:
Martin, Paul D.
    Messengers to the brain.
    (Books for world explorers)
    Bibliography: p.
    Includes index.
    SUMMARY: Describes the workings of the sense organs and explains how the brain and nerves receive and process their messages.
    1. Senses and sensation—Juvenile literature. 2. Sense-organs—Juvenile literature. 3. Brain—Juvenile literature. [1. Senses and sensation. 2. Sense organs. 3. Brain] I. Title. II. Series.
QP434.M37 1984   612.8   82-45636
ISBN 0-87044-499-9 (regular edition)
ISBN 0-87044-504-9 (library edition)

MESSENGERS TO THE BRAIN
Our Fantastic Five Senses
By Paul D. Martin

PUBLISHED BY
THE NATIONAL GEOGRAPHIC SOCIETY
WASHINGTON, D. C.

Gilbert M. Grosvenor, *President*
Melvin M. Payne, *Chairman of the Board*
Owen R. Anderson, *Executive Vice President*
Robert L. Breeden, *Vice President,*
Publications and Educational Media

PREPARED BY THE SPECIAL PUBLICATIONS AND SCHOOL SERVICES DIVISION

Donald J. Crump, *Director*
Philip B. Silcott, *Associate Director*
William L. Allen, William R. Gray, *Assistant Directors*

STAFF FOR BOOKS FOR WORLD EXPLORERS

Ralph Gray, *Editor*
Pat Robbins, *Managing Editor*
Ursula Perrin Vosseler, *Art Director*

STAFF FOR *MESSENGERS TO THE BRAIN*

Margaret McKelway, *Managing Editor*
David P. Johnson, *Picture Editor*
Drayton Hawkins, *Designer*
Debra A. Antonini, Donna B. Kerfoot, *Researchers*
Katherine R. Leitch, *Editorial Assistant*
Artemis S. Lampathakis, *Illustrations Assistant*
Janet A. Dustin, *Art Secretary*

STAFF FOR *FAR-OUT FUN!*

Patricia N. Holland, *Project Editor;* Pat Robbins, *Text Editor;* Debra A. Antonini, Donna B. Kerfoot, *Researchers;* Ursula Perrin Vosseler, *Designer;* Andrea Eberbach/Carol Bancroft and Friends, *Artist*

ENGRAVING, PRINTING, AND PRODUCT MANUFACTURE

Robert W. Messer, *Manager;* George V. White, *Production Manager;* George J. Zeller, Jr., *Production Project Manager;* Mark R. Dunlevy, David V. Showers, Gregory Storer, *Assistant Production Managers;* Mary A. Bennett, *Production Assistant;* Julia F. Warner, *Production Staff Assistant*

STAFF ASSISTANTS: Nancy F. Berry, Pamela A. Black, Mary Frances Brennan, Dianne T. Craven, Carol R. Curtis, Lori E. Davie, Mary Elizabeth Davis, Rosamund Garner, Victoria D. Garrett, Nancy J. Harvey, Sandra K. Huhn, Joan Hurst, Mary Evelyn McKinney, Cleo Petroff, Sheryl A. Prohovich, Kathleen T. Shea, Linda L. Whittington, Virginia A. Williams

MARKET RESEARCH: Mark W. Brown, Joseph S. Fowler, Carrla L. Holmes, Meg McElligott Kieffer, Nancy Serbin, Susan D. Snell, Barbara G. Steinwurtzel

INDEX: Martha K. Hightower

Composition for MESSENGERS TO THE BRAIN by Composition Systems Inc., Falls Church, Va., and National Geographic's Photographic Services, Carl M. Shrader, Director; Lawrence F. Ludwig, Assistant Director. Printed and bound by Holladay-Tyler Printing Corp., Rockville, Md. *Far-out Fun!* booklet and poster printed by McCollum Press, Rockville, Md. Color separations by the Lanman-Progressive Co., Washington, D. C.; Lincoln Graphics, Inc., Cherry Hill, N.J.; NEC, Inc., Nashville, Tenn. *Classroom Activities* folder produced by Mazer Corp., Dayton, Ohio.